THE WAKE FOREST SERIES OF

IRISH POETRY   VOLUME THREE

THE WAKE FOREST SERIES OF

irish poetry

COLETTE BRYCE, JUSTIN QUINN,

JOHN MCAULIFFE, MAURICE RIORDAN,

AND GERARD FANNING

SELECTED, WITH A PREFACE

AND INTERVIEWS BY

CONOR O'CALLAGHAN

WAKE FOREST UNIVERSITY PRESS

Copyright © 2013 by

Wake Forest University Press

Preface by Conor O'Callaghan copyright © 2013

Interviews copyright © 2013 by

Conor O'Callaghan and respective poets

All rights reserved

For permission to reproduce or

broadcast these poems, write to:

Wake Forest University Press

Post Office Box 7333

Winston-Salem, NC 27109

Designed by Quemadura and typeset

in Ariston, Eurostile, and Trinité

Printed on acid-free, recycled paper

in the United States of America

LCCN 2013937139

ISBN 978-1-930630-64-2

Wake Forest University Press

www.wfu.edu/wfupress

Publication of this book was

generously supported by

the Boyle Family Fund.

CONTENTS

Justin Quinn

NEW POEM

Nostalgia 90

John McAuliffe

INTERVIEW 93

Maurice Riordan

Gerard Fanning

It is difficult to put an exact time-scale on the work gathered in these pages. The earliest book selected from is Gerard Fanning's *Easter Snow*, which appeared in 1992. Both Maurice Riordan and Justin Quinn would publish their respective first collections in 1995. Both Fanning and Riordan were in their forties when their first books came out, and some of their work here may well date from the 1980s. At the other end of the scale, the most recent work by Quinn, Colette Bryce and John McAuliffe dates from 2011. Let's just say that this work, give or take a few years and exceptions, happened in a two-decade period from the early 1990s onwards.

In that two-decade period, both culturally and economically, Ireland changed. After decades of mass unemployment and emigration, and thanks to funding from the European Union, infrastructural agreements in the public sector and tax incentives for multi-nationals to relocate on our shores, Ireland's economy grew dramatically and very suddenly. In a "quality of life" league table published by *The Economist* in 2004, Ireland was deemed the best place in the world to live. By 2007 we were officially the richest country in Europe and the second only to Japan globally.

One common thesis argues that Ireland's boom was due in no small part to the legalization of contraception, which occurred only in 1983. The average family-size plummeted and, with it, expendable income rose. As a result, this twenty year period was one of secularization and consumerist materialism. Where a century previously their forefathers had formed the Land Leagues to reclaim and distribute Anglo-Irish estates, Irish men and women became obsessive about real estate. One's prosperity, one's standing in the world, seemed to be measured exclusively by volume of investment property acquired both at home and on in Europe.

In addition to contraception, legislation around abortion was softened in the wake of the infamous "X Case". Pornography was also legalized for sale on shop shelves. The vice-like grip that the Catholic Church had on the State and its population was loosening for good. In 1993 homosexuality was finally decriminalized. The case of Father Brendan Smyth in 1994, a priest eventually imprisoned for pederast acts, initiated a spate of similar convictions. The Smyth case even brought down one of many coalition governments of this period, after the processing of papers for his extradition to Northern Ireland was delayed in suspicious circumstances in the South.

The IRA called a ceasefire in 1993, thus beginning the end of North Ireland's so-called "Troubles". President Bill Clinton made two state visits in the nineties.

In 1993 Roddy Doyle won the Booker Prize for his fictional portrayal of Dublin's inner city. In 1995 Seamus Heaney won a Nobel Prize for Literature. We won the Eurovision Song Contest in three successive years. In U2, we had the biggest stadium rock group in the world. We seemed, also, to manufacture boy-band hit-machines at will. We had cash and we had caché. Being Irish had become socially acceptable, a source of pride even, downright cool.

It is equally difficult to find direct correlations between such social forces and the poems included here, and foolish even to attempt that. Poetry continues to happen, as it should, in silence and solitude. That remains as true of the work of the poets of this post-Troubles, Celtic Tiger generation as it ever was. However, those events and changes are often visible and audible as background. There is also here, I suggest, a delectation of the material surface, of bric-a-brac and brands, that is absolutely of the age. Subjects that would have seemed unimaginable to their immediate predecessors—trips to IKEA, credit cards, plasma screens and Japanese cinema—are second nature to these poets. Not that any of these poems are ultimately *about* any of these things. Rather, they use the data and white noise of 21st century life as subjects for coming at poetry's old enduring themes from different angles.

Foolish, too, to attempt to establish connections between these poets. The only real connections between these poets and their work are their Irishness, their mutual inclusion in this book and the fact that four of five have made their homes outside Ireland. The different landscapes that each inhabits is everywhere obvious in the work and obviously not Ireland. Each, it would appear, has long since got beyond the jaded fixities of land and history and faith and nationhood, what Patrick Kavanagh sarcastically and correctly termed 'the Irish thing'; and each neither sentimentalizes nor elegizes his/her 'exile'. For them, living abroad is a cultural preference rather than an economic necessity.

But for obvious illustrious exceptions, the bulk of poetry written and published in Ireland in the 1980s could be loosely characterized as a form of expressive, quasi-mystical, affirmative free verse. It was, truth to tell, scarcely worthy of the term. If the poets here are collectively indicative of any one thing in Irish poetry, it is of a reaction that occurred gradually towards greater formal determinism, a more international perspective, empiricism, rationalism and wit.

This reaction, or shift, is perhaps best exemplified by the ten issues of Metre (1996-2005), an intelligent and entertaining magazine edited by Justin Quinn and David Wheatley. At times, possibly, like all reactions, this one exceeded its sell-by date. The emphasis on rationalism and formalism resulted in a lot of half-rhyming verse devoid of risk or sensual excitement. Yet, much as a gifted generation of poets was doing in the UK at the same time, these poets generally breathed fresh air into the fools' echo chamber that poetry in Ireland had surely become. If post-modernism means anything, it means choosing one's own tradition from whatever source.

Justin Quinn and John McAuliffe, perhaps, best epitomize this shift. Born and raised in south Dublin, Quinn moved to Prague in 1993, and still lives there with his Czech wife and sons. His refusal to read Irish paradigms out of his poems, coupled with his desire herein expressed to be interred finally in Czech soil, feel pointed. The brilliant cerebral formalism of Quinn's work seems to owe more to American exemplars such as Richard Wilbur and Anthony Hecht than any Irish predecessors. McAuliffe has lived in the UK for most of his adult life, initially in London, and now co-directs the Centre for New Writing at the University of Manchester. Like Quinn, McAuliffe is an active critic. Though often obviously more 'Irish' in subject matter, McAuliffe's best poems bear little resemblance in tone and style to that of peers still based in Ireland. His beautiful 'Today's Imperative', for example, updates Horace's *carpe diem* insistence for the age of affluence. Even his 'Aerialist', perhaps the most overtly Celtic Tiger poem in the whole anthology, has the associative propulsion and range of August Kleinzahler or a young John Ashbery.

Raised in rural Cork and tutored by John Montague in UCC, Maurice Riordan has lived in London since the early 1980s and is established in that context. He has published three collections with Faber & Faber (a fourth is forthcoming) and edits *Poetry Review*, the journal of the Poetry Society. Riordan's internationalism surfaces in his interest in contemporary science, and in his attempts to quantify time and space in imagery. However frequently his work returns to his childhood landscape, it does so in unexpected modes, such as the prose glosses of 'The Idylls'. Colette Bryce has been based in the UK much of her adult life. She succeeded Riordan as editor of *Poetry London* and has published three collections with Picador. Her work, with its winning combination of sensuousness and skepticism, seems intent on exorcising the childhood trauma of the Troubles and entering realms of experience new to the Irish lyric. Only Gerard Fanning still lives in Ireland. Even Fanning, however, enjoys something of the 'inner émigré' predicament that Trotsky coined and Seamus Heaney adopted. He belongs to that shadowy enclave of civil servant poets, for whom poetry exists as a silent subversion. He does not, that I know of, participate in any 'scene', and instead writes gorgeous cryptic narratives that read like pint-sized spy thrillers where protagonists travel incognito or disappear altogether.

Each poet is represented by selections from all of their published collections, and by some new previously uncollected work into the bargain. Rather than attempting to describe their work at length in this preface, I have chosen to conduct interviews via email specific to the poems included. They are far more eloquent about their own work than I could hope to be. I am grateful to each of them for the generosity of their answers, and for their patience with the editor throughout this process.

We have come full circle. The bubble burst and Ireland, at the time of writing, is repaying an unfathomable bailout from the International Monetary Fund, subject to an enforced austerity regime. Unemployment is at fifteen percent. Most of our immigrants have returned home. Since 2006, for taxation purposes, U2 have been registered in the Netherlands. Their debut at the Glastonbury Festival in July 2011, around about the same time that the most recent of these poems were being written, was subject to protests against their perceived tax avoidance. Now even U2, so often symbolic of a new confident Ireland, have gone Dutch.

CONOR O'CALLAGHAN
SAN MARTINO IN COLLE OCTOBER 2012

Colette Bryce

By way of background, what is the earliest poem in this selection? Can you remember when and where it was written, and in what spirit? More particularly, what do you recall of Ireland/Britain and their poetry at the moment of composition, and of how you defined your creative ambitions starting out?

I think that the poem 'Itch' probably dates back to 1992–93, when I had just been converted to contemporary poetry. Prior to that, I had undergone a long, hardly noticeable, de-conversion from Catholicism. I was living in a shared house in North London. Looking at 'Itch' now, I realize that I must have written it in the year or two between 'coming out' and the dreaded instance of telling my mother. My mother really did suffer from ear itch. She used to go after it with a hair clip!

The poetry scene that I was exposed to initially would have involved younger poets from around the UK, and especially the "New Generation" who were promoted in the media the following year. Contemporary poetry seemed to be thriving, and inclusive, and the truth is I was in love with it. I had a tremendous sense of vocation: this is what I will do and it doesn't matter if I'm not successful. At that time, being Irish in London didn't seem important, and I didn't think of myself in relation to the Irish tradition at all. Poetry belonged to the now and the future, and of course that would change in the years to come. I read everything I could find.

When you call 'Itch' a coming out poem, do you mean in terms of sexuality or poetry or both? And in what sense is the poem's narrative one of coming out? It seems to be as much about your mother failing to hear. More specifically, the influences from that group would be Carol Ann Duffy, Simon Armitage? The development of idiom into metaphor, and the street-wise hit-and-miss internal rhymes . . .

It's not a coming out poem as such, more a playful take on who we are versus who we're supposed to be, in our parents' eyes (ears?), and how religious interference can deafen people to real experience. Coming out as a poet? Yes, I like that way of putting it; that can be more disappointing to parents than anything else we might throw at them.

At that time, I wanted to read about women's experience in poetry, and also working class experience, and Carol Ann Duffy's work offered those connections. I was impressed by the work of the Scottish poets Don Paterson and Kathleen Jamie as well, and many others from the generation above them, the Irish poets Paul Durcan and Brendan Kennelly, for example. The 'New Gen' was only one aspect, the younger, more visible scene if you like. I was also seeking out a female line in poetry, as this hadn't been on offer in my education. Elizabeth Bishop famously refused to have her work included in women's anthologies, for valid reasons, but those anthologies were important to me when starting out, as a shortcut to the invisible. I was finding my way to the previous generations, and to the work of European and American women poets. Sharon Olds was a discovery for me at that time, with her powerful first book *Satan Says*, and I've continued to read her work over the years.

Before we talk about 'Footings', 'Line,' and 'Break', can I ask you to describe for a US audience Derry and your childhood there in the 70s and 80s? It's like poetry's equivalent of being born with a silver spoon in your mouth! What was going on and how aware were you, if at all, of the great generation of poets writing through the Troubles?

It wouldn't be my idea of a silver spoon, more of a plastic fork! I suppose those well-documented images of The Troubles, of rioting and barricades, the hunger strikes and British army patrols, pretty much conjure up the atmosphere. I lived in the Bogside area of Derry that saw a lot of the trouble. My mother had been caught up in the civil rights shootings on Bloody Sunday, and we grew up firmly rooted in the republican tradition. Public demonstrations were a regular part of life: protest marches, memorials, and funerals. The church was the other thread: the church and political calendars would structure the year.

I wasn't aware of contemporary Irish poetry as a teenager, or of the Belfast poets who were grappling with those events as they unfolded. At the all-girls school that I attended, we were issued with an all-male poetry anthology in which the scattering of 20th century work had a distinctly rural theme. I remember 'Cynddylan on a Tractor' by the Welsh poet R S Thomas as perhaps the only contemporary poem we read. It's a good poem, mind you.

The first three poems of your first book all contain boundaries and barriers. Were these divisions actual or imaginative? 'Footings', ostensibly a simple narrative about two girls daring one another to jump from a wall, seems to be about overcoming received prejudice. Is this fair, or is it a simplistic lens through which every Northern Irish poem gets viewed? The poem even has a lane 'yeared into two deep tracks' . . .

It seems to be about action and consequence, two ways of doing things. One child can see that the other will injure herself by standing up and leaping off the high wall, but a question mark remains as to whether persuasion, even logic, might have changed her course of action. One could certainly bring a political reading to that, but you're right in saying that this can become a default lens.

Is it the case that you intended to write poems about lines of division, or realized after their completion that this had happened? In 'Line,' there is the actual sectarian divide in the city. But the line seems to be also that of poetry, and possibly a point of connection as well as division? The 'Line' is capitalized and addressed in the second person.

In those days, and I suppose to some extent it is still true, I never intended to write a poem *about* something. I was surprised, and grateful, when a poem emerged, and then I would try to find out what it was doing, and attempt to realize it better. 'Line,' begins with a childish visual fantasy of the line taking on a life of its own and snaking away through the city. I can recognise, in the early poems (and this won't necessarily come across to the reader), the geography of where I was positioned; our street overlooked a valley so we could see over the city from the top windows. You could imagine the city as a maze. I could see across the valley of the Bogside to the ancient Derry walls, a British army post in those days, so you had a sense of very strong boundaries between communities. 'Line,' starts with an innocent parental boundary and then it moves off mischievously, and then into history. Derry had of course been cordoned off in the Boundary Commission, so the British army checkpoints on the roads out of town were part of our daily life. The border was the primary line in all our minds.

The title of 'Break' seems to pun on, again, division and a soldier's pause for rest on another wall. What was your thinking, do you recall, in using a nursery rhyme metre?

The metre is intended to convey the child's perspective and voice in the first eight lines. There's a shift in tense in the ninth line where the speaker's adult perspective comes in. The poem was based on a real incident where I was marched up the street by the shopkeeper and the soldier was told in no uncertain terms what he could do with his money. The true errand had been for 'pop'. In Derry we used the word "lemonade" for all soft drinks, so it was the word that gave me away. I didn't even know what pop was! The shopkeeper's husband was a political prisoner. As children we would be naturally curious about the soldiers—most of them were very young—while they were on foot patrol in our streets.

The brilliant poem 'Form' seems viewable through two competing default lenses: politics and gender. I've heard you assert in readings that the poem is definitely not about anorexia, but rather about self-styled hunger artists. Also, surely the poem is partly informed by the experience of living through the Hunger Strikes of 1981? Clearly not about them, but poems carry baggage forward often without our realizing it. Much as Muldoon's great poems 'Gathering Mushrooms' and 'Christo's' are not about the Hunger Strikes, but seem saturated by that collective experience.

I probably did more reading around 'Form' than for any poem I've written. I was exploring the subject of hunger, or self-starvation, in many directions, from the Suffragettes to fasting ascetics, and the experience of the hunger strikers would have been part of that. I was interested in the historical phenomena of hunger artists, who would starve themselves as a kind of occupation or art, in fairgrounds for example. The eventual writing process was an exploration and the character's voice, and truth, evolved. I'm surprised that it ended up being only one poem because it was an intellectual process that I was involved in for quite a while.

My intention wasn't to write an anorexia poem, and I think if I had had that agenda it would have failed because anorexia eludes easy explanation. And yet, readers with that experience have brought a lot to my poem and it is a reading that clearly offers itself. I was fascinated by the symbolism of eating—I think Susie Orbach noted this—of how we accept the world through literally taking it into our bodies as food. She wrote about the sense of refusal in the anorexic, and the symbolism of that, and I found that idea of refusal very powerful. This connected for me with the absolute quality there is to art and to writing.

The time of the hunger strikes was a fraught period in our lives in Derry. They seemed to extend for a very long time and there was a billboard in the centre of town displaying a terrible countdown, ostensibly of the days since the strikes began, but in reality, to each man's death. I remember attending the funeral of Patsy O'Hara, the young prisoner from Derry who died. I would have been eleven years old at the time and I don't know how we began to process those events, as children.

Those other poems selected from the first book—'Wish You Were', 'Phone', 'Young', and 'Nevers'—all have a gorgeous feel of heady youthful passions to them. Can I ask you to say something about writing love poetry, and how you use communication devices like postcard and phones? Also, given the book's title and its final poem 'Nevers', there does seem to be a reconciliation with Catholicism, its idea of passion if not the actual faith.

I suppose in the same way as happiness 'writes white', love poetry seems to thrive on the irreconcilable variety; those particular poems all circle around a kind of longing. 'Wish You Were', for example, could equally be addressed to a lover or to the possibility of love itself. In a later poem, 'The Poetry Bug', the love poem adopts, rather horribly, the form of a dust mite. The postcards and long-distance phonecalls recall the geography of that time, the immigrant Londoner's sense of travelling without moving, and the emigrant's sense of dislocation. My first partner was Spanish and we lived in Spain for a while during the writing of that book, so that was another flag-pin on the map of that time.

Yes, the Catholic imagery was, and is, a rich source. A book about incorruptible flesh, and ideas of sainthood, led eventually to 'Nevers', and back again to the subject of irreconcilable love. I think poetry is a 'faithful' art and is perhaps not ever wholly accessed from one's most rational thought.

Your second collection, The Full Indian Rope Trick, *seems even more concerned with home and escaping it. Where the title poem, which won the British National Poetry Competition, imagines magicking out of central Derry, the final poem '+' admits 'we . . . haven't taken off at all' and lands right back into 'Irish rain'. Does every poet have material that is inescapable?*

Most of us would have to confess to particular obsessions, I suppose. 'Mad Ireland hurt you into poetry', wrote Auden of Yeats, and perhaps mad Ireland will always be inescapable for emigrant poets like ourselves, Conor. I've travelled around a lot since I left Ireland at 18, and I've lived in a number of cities. There's been a price to pay for all of that moving around, but there's also been a lot to gain, from the places and people. Emigration was and is a key experience in my life . . . not a single experience but a continuous one. The idea of home grows ever more elusive.

Other poems in the first section of the book recall growing up in the sectarian divide. '1981' returns once again to the year of the Hunger Strikes. Do poems about the Troubles by poets of our generation, do you think, differ from poems dealing with the same material by the previous generation?

That's a good question and I think it still remains to be seen. Poets of our generation are only now finding strategies to write about what happened, because in some ways it can almost seem to be off limits, as if it is already written. But of course our lives are not written, and growing up in that war is something that is—looking back to your last question—inescapable. I liked the statement from Picasso that Medbh McGuckian used as epigraph to one of her collections: 'I have not painted the war . . . but I have no doubt that the war is in . . . these paintings I have done.' I find it can't be approached very deliberately.

'Song for a Stone' and 'Words and Music' are two beautiful poems of love and love lost at the end of the book. How important is music to you? On the evidence of your poems, you have a very pure ear. Also, the love poems seem to set up this parallel universe in your work: there is home with all its complications of the past and religion and sectarian conflict, and there is this mini republic of love that is free of all of that.

I mentioned earlier that I see poetry as a faithful kind of art, and I think faith in love, the idea of love as a solution, can be the thing that guides us in our twenties and early thirties. The music is all-important to me. Whoever it was said 'prose is to poetry as walking is to dancing' got it right—I think poetry does make language dance. I love all of the devices, the tricks and techniques we employ to make words dance, to make the music be heard in the reader's inner ear.

Moving on to the third book, Self-Portrait in the Dark, I'm struck by the feel of your poems talking to one another. Where '+' is about flying home, here we find a poem called 'When I land in Northern Ireland' about that same magnetic pull. That latter poem is especially tough: you use the common Irish offer of a drink 'What's your poison?' with real venom!

Oh dear, there was no venom intended, perhaps it's the word 'poison' sounding too loudly? The colloquial offer of a drink in a bar takes the speaker's mind off somewhere else, towards the poison (or poisoned chalice), yes. The 'stratus shadows darkening the crops', seen from the plane, are connecting now in my mind with a famous Marlboro cigarette advert that played with a similar image of shadows moving over a landscape. Some people argued it was employing reverse psychology, conjuring up images of disease in order to induce greater denial in the smoker. (I've just tried to Google the advert, to no avail, but in the process I learned that three actors who played the Marlboro man eventually died of lung cancer!). Sorry, a tangent . . .

Regarding poems talking to one another, I think yes, increasingly they do. I didn't always see the connections when I was younger, especially in my first book, which had developed over a longer period of time. With subsequent collections, the poems tend to be written within a few years of each other, and there is a greater sense of conversation happening between them. Putting a book together gets more interesting as you go on, as a poet, when you're more in tune with these relationships and happy to help them along.

Similarly, 'Finisterre' feels like an updating of 'Nevers': the title, the setting . . . But where the earlier poem is about youthful passion, this feels wiser and more solitary. 'Finisterre' reminds me of Elizabeth Bishop's great late poem 'The End of March'.

I should probably point out to the readers of this anthology that *Self-Portrait in the Dark* was written at the end of a ten-year relationship, so that had some bearing on the mood of the collection. There's a low-lit sort of atmosphere throughout, and several poems are set at night. 'Aloneness' as a word interested me: its difference from solitude, so necessary for poetry, and from loneliness, an occupational hazard. Aloneness seemed to describe that sense of being an individual in the world, that is felt newly and keenly when one leaves a pairing. Finisterre of course is the peninsula in Northern Spain to which pilgrims sometimes walk after completing the longer trek along the Camino de Santiago, to the town of Santiago de Compostela. It is literally 'the end of the earth'. I walked from León to Santiago in 2005, and visited Finisterre, so this poem was directly inspired by the place. I love Elizabeth Bishop's poem 'The End of March'. Bishop famously called herself 'the loneliest person who ever lived', and her rootlessness seems connected to her incredible clear-sightedness.

'Where Are You?' echoes earlier poems in its use of the phone. But more than that, there seems to be an obsession with fragmentation here. 'Self-Portrait in a Broken Wing Mirror' pieces together a sort of cubist self, and 'Where Are You?' identifies a loved one's whereabouts through scraps of sound. Given the book's title, and these poems, are you saying that one's identity can never be whole or clear?

I couldn't assert anything much about such a slippery thing as identity. The book's title *Self-Portrait in the Dark* is of course almost a disclaimer; it cancels itself out because the portrait is either veiled in darkness, or the portraitist cannot see what she seeks to depict. We do have this fragmentation of sounds, and visuals, in the two poems you mention, and elsewhere. In the latter poem, with the broken wing mirror, the speaker is at the scene of a car crash and is, as far as I can tell, speaking/thinking after death.

Much of your later work seems to be about language and poetry in particular. Don't poets always worry about navel-gazing in this regard?! I am thinking especially of 'Sin Música' and 'The Poetry Bug', where love and poetry seem to act as metaphors for one another as they have done down through the ages. I've heard you talk in the past about Donne's 'The Flea'. Is this somewhere in the wings of 'The Poetry Bug'?

Yes, there's always a danger. Some critics would suggest that all poems are somehow 'about' poetry, and there are others, like the late Michael

Donaghy, who considered a poem about poetry to be a good cue for taking a cold shower. 'Sin Música' was a little experiment in the villanelle form. I was trying to do something a little more flexible with the form, but the subject relates to an earlier love poem you've mentioned 'Words and Music', where the phrase 'words, words, words!' is spoken by the lover as a kind of admonishment. The poems are situated at the beginning and end of a relationship, and we meet 'words, words; / words' again, as if it all comes back to there. It's funny that you ask is Donne's flea lurking behind the 'Poetry Bug' because of course it must be but I had genuinely never entertained the thought on a conscious level. I can't remember when you might have heard me talk about the poem—it feels like a long time since I've engaged with it, but it's nice to think that it's in there.

Can I ask you to say something about the uncollected poems here, 'Boredoom' and 'Jean'? I am struck at how even secular things become prayers in your work, and how the plural 'we' inevitably narrows into a very singular 'I'?

I grew up in a large group of siblings—there were nine of us—so the sense of collective identity was strong. Often when I talk about childhood I talk about 'we', my sisters and I: *we felt this, we experienced that . . .* It's interesting looking again at 'Boredoom' how the 'I' emerges out of that place and into the future, with the idea of a name called from a yard, a naming, and a sense of an identity forming.

The word 'Boredoom' was a misprint in an email from a friend, which seemed to conjure up those long summers of creative boredom in childhood, married to that Cold War nervousness around the nuclear bomb (not to mention our Catholic end-of-the-world fantasies!), hence the doom. The poem 'Jean' is a relatively recent poem. I always remembered Jean Rhys's devastating response to her late success after the publication of *The Wide Sargasso Sea*, 'It has come too late'.

She had suffered a great deal. Jean Rhys is one of my favourite prose writers. I've been drawn to her characters, as in *Good Morning, Midnight* and her other novels of that time.

How do you write poems? Practically, how do you go about it? How does it begin and how long does it take?

I suppose I have to have a little something to go on, to begin with: a phrase, an image, or just a scrap of an idea that I have a strong sense will open up to reveal a greater imaginative space. So to begin with it's a note-taking process. Sometimes I like to work on a big sheet of paper and spider off in all directions, other times I'll be working on the back of an envelope. But for me it's always a physical process, something that happens between the brain and the arm and the pen, and the physical act of handwriting enables the poem to grow.

I think these days, which are probably only the embryonic days of computers, one of the drawbacks is the linearity of the document. For me, poetry doesn't get written in straight lines, or from the top of a page to the bottom. It definitely gets written in little explosions, or clusters. I think if I were to write straight into Word for Windows, the poems might end up as predictable as the format implies.

A poem—and I'm generalizing greatly here—will take me the bones of a week, initially, during which I'll work through up to twenty drafts, but then I'll return to it later many times, and often there's a niggling problem that doesn't get resolved for a long time, something rhythmical or imprecise. I'll not publish a poem for at least a year, usually several. You have to fall out of love with it.

FOOTINGS

You could see, for the life of you, no clear point
in monkeying seven, eight feet to the ground;
to slide from the belly, swing there (caught
by the arms, by the palms, by the fingertips), drop.
If I'd taken the trouble of minuses, pluses,
the length of the body, the height of the wall,
even pushed myself to prediction, scared you;
as it stood, before you leapt, I dared you.

And the lane it was yeared into two deep tracks
as we found our feet in the lengthened light,
for those with the leap approach to life,
for those who measure, look, think twice.
Both of us sobbing, I shouldered you home
with your hard-won knowledge, broken bone.

LINE,

you were drawn in the voice of my mother;
not past Breslin's, don't step over.
Saturday border, breach in the slabs,
creep to the right, Line,
sidelong, crab,

cut up the tarmac, sunder the flowers,
drop like an anchor,
land in The Moor as a stringball

ravelling under the traffic,
up, you're the guttering scaling McCafferty's,

maze through the slating,
dive from sight and down into history, Line,
take flight in the chase of the fences,
leap the streets
where lines will meet you, race you, lead

you into the criss-crossed heart of the city
of lines for the glory, lines for the pity.

BREAK

Soldier boy, dark and tall, sat for a rest
on Crumlish's wall. *Come on over.*

Look at my Miraculous Medal.
Let me punch your bulletproof vest. *Go on, try.*

The gun on your knees is blackened metal.
Here's the place where the bullets sleep.

Here's the catch and here's the trigger.
Let me look through the eye.

Soldier, you sent me for cigs but a woman
came back and threw the money in your face.

I watched you backtrack, alter, cover
your range of vision, shoulder to shoulder.

ITCH

I believe that Jesus lives
deep in the ditch of my mother's ear,

an unreachable itch that never leaves.
And I believe when Jesus breathes

a million microscopic hairs
lean in the breeze like sapling trees.

Things I begin to tell her,
I believe sometimes she cannot hear

for the whispering like wishes
of Jesus softly breathing there.

FORM

For some time I have been starving myself,
and not in the interest of fashion,
but because it is something to do
and I do it well.

I'm writing this as my only witness
has been the glass on the wall.
Someone must know what I've done
and there's no one to tell.

Commitment is the main thing. After this,
the emptiness, the hunger isn't a sacrifice

but a tool. I found I was gifted, good.
And full of my vocation, sat or stood

at the mirror just watching my work
take shape, conform to my critical eye.
Or would lie, supine, stomach shrinking,
contracting, perfecting its concave line.

Each day gave a little more: depth to the shallows
of the temples, definition to the cheek,
contrast to the clavicle, the ankle bone, the rib,
the raised X-ray perception of my feet.

But one night I dressed and went for a walk
and felt a latent contamination of eyes
from windows and cars. I'd been feeling
strange, somehow encased, the hollow rush

of my own breath like tides in the shell
of my own head. A woman passed
and I saw myself in her glance,
her expression blank as a future.

The next day I woke to double vision,
everything suddenly terribly clear, only twinned.
My hearing, too, was distracted.
I sipped some water and retched.

My speech, when I test it, has stretched
to a distant slur like a voice from behind a door.
I would think I was losing my mind
if it wasn't behind all this from the start.

Tonight there's an almost imperceptible buzzing
in my bones, like the sound of electric razors,
a lawn-mower several gardens down.
I worry that they're crumbling

under my skin, dissolving like aspirin.
I worry that my bones are caving in.
When I sit my joints begin to set.
I try to stand and I'm hit by a shift in gravity,

the point where an aircraft lifts and enters flight.
And I think my sight is burning out.
I think it is losing its pupil heart.
Objects are calmly vacating their outlines,

colours slowly absorbing the dark.
In my dream the shovels uncover a hare,
preserved in its form, its self-shaped lair,
and I'm travelling in. There is no going back.

WISH YOU WERE

Here, an aftertaste of traffic taints
the city's breath, as mornings
yawn and bare this street

like teeth. Here, airplanes leaving
Heathrow scare this house
to trembling; these rooms protect

their space with outstretched walls,
and wait. And evenings fall
like discs in a jukebox, playing

a song called *Here*, night after night.
Wish you were. Your postcards
land in my hall like meteorites.

PHONE

Though we've come to hate this line
we call; stuck evenings when we've dried
the well of talk, we bide the time
in small long-distance silences
and lend ourselves as audience
to voices washed from tense to tense
across the middle air.

So, often, more than I can bear,
missing you brings this desire
at least to hear and to be heard
and then, there's something to be said
for this. For this becomes a web,
becomes a hair, a strength, a thread,
a harness between us, in all fairness,
you in my hereness, me in your thereness.

YOUNG

Loose stacks of cassettes collapse
to the slam of the door behind us.
We take the stairs
in twos and threes,

we don't know where we might be
this time next year,
but meanwhile,
we apply to the future in lunch-breaks;

taste the possibility, the sweet adhesive
strip of A4 envelopes on tongues,
punch the day and run
to post, to home, and out.

We eye each other up as future lovers;
our faces smooth as blank maps
of undiscovered countries,
where only we might go.

We mean to go, we thumb the guides,
we spin the globe and halt it
at Calcutta, then Alaska, now Japan,
and plan. Imagine.

Not for us the paper lanterns of remember,
but the hard bright bulbs of sheer want.
We reminisce at length
about the future, which is better;

we harbour it in our hearts
like a terrible crush. We laugh
and drink to this in rented rooms.
We think Not this, but older, elsewhere, soon.

NEVERS

Passions never spoken,
never broken but preserved,
never layered under marriages
or burnt to dust by fast affairs
are saints to us,

the sacred ones,
bodily enshrined
to lie in state like Bernadette
at Nevers of the mind;
amazing, garlanded and fair.

Older, at the inkling
of an accent or a smile,
we travel there.

STONES

We kept ourselves from children who were rich,
who were shaped in the folds of newest clothes,
who were strapped in the backs of foreign cars

whose quick electric windows rose
effortlessly, that poured into the stream of traffic;

but stared, fascinated, at their orthodontic
iron smiles, their nerve-averted eyes.

They were quiet. They feared rain. They were taught
to recite in yellow rooms *Colette, Suzette,*
Jo-jo and Lou are coming here for tea . . .
or to sing at the prompt of a tuning fork
How merry your life must be . . . ,

they had no idea, but disappeared
to the south of France twice a year—
as we ran the streets, the lanes and squares,
a band of outlaws, ne'er-do-wells
—then left for schools we didn't know.

From walls we saw them come and go.
War-daubed faces, feathers in our hair, wild,

we never smiled.

SATELLITE

For all we see of you these days,
you might be living in outer space!
shouted my mother,
after my father, table cleared

of dinner plates, had poured a sea
of silver and coppers, metalfalls
from the money-drawer of the pub
where he'd spent the night before
pulling pints for the late drinkers.

We, his band of little helpers,
counted them into cityscapes
of stacks and towers—hours of fun—
our hands would turn an alien green
as, through the wall, their arguing
went on, my father circling,
there's nothing left
in this doom town for us;
my mother stood her ground.

Part of the task was to separate
the rogue harps and leaping fish
from the Queen's heads; the odd button;
even an errant dime or quarter
that had found its way across the water
bearing, on the backward swell
of the great Atlantic wishing well,
via the till of the Telstar Bar,
news of Brooklyn, or Manhattan.

And so, strangely enough, to Florida.
Twenty from our side of the River
Foyle and twenty more from the other,
lifted out of a 'war-torn community'
to mix three weeks in a normal society.
That was the general idea.

When we arrived we were paired
and placed with a host couple, good
church people, settled and stable.
She was the first Prod I had ever met;
a small girl, pale and introvert, who wept
for home, then sniffed, and smiled.

The husband sat at the head of the table
holding forth, hot and bothered.
He couldn't decide on the right word,
hmmed and hawed between Blacks and Coloured,
whatever, his point? They were bone idle,
wouldn't accept the jobs they were offered.

The woman dreamed of having a child.
I took to the role of living doll
and would tolerate each morning's session
under the tug of curling tongs.
I had never even heard of Racism.
We gave a concert on the last night,

forty of us, rigid with stage fright.
My whistle shrieked on a high note.
We harmonized on all the songs
but fell apart with the grand finale,
the well-rehearsed 'O I know a wee spot . . .'
as the group split between London and Lovely.

1981

A makeshift notice in the square
says it with numbers, each day higher.
North of here, in a maze of cells,
a man cowers, says it with hunger,
skin, bone, wrought to a bare
statement. Waiting, there are others.

Days give on to days; we stall
in twos and threes in the town centre,
talk it over, say it with anger,
What's the news? It's no better.
Headlines on the evening paper
spell it out in huge letters.

Over graves and funeral cars
the vast bays of colour say it
with flowers, flowers everywhere;
heads are bowed, as mute as theirs,
that will find a voice in the darker hours,
say it with stones, say it with fire.

THE FULL INDIAN ROPE TRICK

There was no secret
murmured down through a long line
of elect; no dark fakir, no flutter
of notes from a pipe,
no proof, no footage of it—
but I did it,

Guildhall Square, noon,
in front of everyone.
There were walls, bells, passers-by;
then a rope, thrown, caught by the sky
and me, young, up and away,
goodbye.

Goodbye, goodbye.
Thin air. First try.
A crowd hushed, squinting eyes
at a full sun. There
on the stones
the slack weight of a rope

coiled in a crate, a braid
eighteen summers long,
and me—
I'm long gone,
my one-off trick
unique, unequalled since.

And what would I tell them
given the chance?
It was painful; it took years.
I'm my own witness,
guardian of the fact
that I'm still here.

SONG FOR A STONE

after Iain Crichton Smith

You are at the bottom of my mind
like a stone dropped once by chance in a pool
to the black belied
by a surface ruled
by total reflection of sky.

I do not have the know of your want or why,
I do not have the know of your way.
I have only the flow
of the come what may
in the light to the front of my liquid eye.

But you have put a sadness in the blue-
green waters of my mind
for as long as we both may live.

For your time is not of the colour of mine
and the name that is on you cannot be written
over these lips in love.

WORDS AND MUSIC

She moves about in the tiny flat
with the long strides of a goddess,
fixing this, or watering that,
mixing the books up, wearing my shirt.

She dials the little radio
through crashing waves of static,
through 'words, words, words!'
and finds a hidden symphony

then moves a chair to occupy
the single square of morning sun,
basks in the full length of herself,
ankles hooked on the window sill,

feet conducting sky. She asks me
if I love her. I wouldn't quite
go that far. It's just that
if she leaves me, I'm done for.

+

Through the cabin window's haze
we watch the black shadow of our plane
free itself from the undercarriage,
separate, then fall away.

With it falls the sunlit runway,
grids of crops and reservoirs, then all
the scattered glitter of a city
falls, the tattered coastline of a country

plunges out of view.
And just when you might expect to see
the globe in brilliant clarity,
cloud fills the tiny screen

and we, who haven't taken off
at all, wait, seatbelts on,
for the world to turn and return to us
as it always does, sooner or later,

to fix itself to the craft again
at a point marked with the shadow of a plane,
pencilled now on a runway, growing
larger under Irish rain.

SELF-PORTRAIT IN A BROKEN WING-MIRROR

The lens has popped from its case,
minutely cracked and yet intact, tilted
where it stopped against a rock on the tarmac.
And this could be Selkirk, washed up on a beach,
in prone position surveying the sweep
of his future sanctuary, or prison.

But no, that's me, a cubist depiction: my ear,
its swirl and ridge of pearly cartilage,
peachy lobe and indent of a piercing
not jewelled for years. I punctured that
with a nerve of steel at fifteen in a bolted
room. It was Hallowe'en. I had no fear.

The ear is parted neatly from the head
by breaks in the glass, a weird mosaic
or logic puzzle for the brain to fix.
The eyebrow, stepped in sections, stops
then starts again, recognisably mine.
The nose, at an intersection of cracks,

is all but lost except for the small sculpted
cave of a shadowy nostril. The eye
is locked on itself, the never-easy gaze
of the portraitist, the hood half open,
the hub of the pupil encircled with green
and a ring of flame. I have make-up on,

a smudging of pencil, brushed black lashes.
I'd swear the face looks younger than before,
the skin sheer, the fine wires of laughter
disappeared without the animation.
The lips are slack, pink, segmented;
a slight gravitational pull towards the earth

gives the upper one a sort of Elvis curl.
The same effect has made the cheek more full.

I have never been so still. A beautiful day
and not another car for what seems like hours.
Also in the glass, bisected, out of focus,
a streamer of road and a third of sky.

Presently, I will attempt to move,
attempt to arise in a shower of diamonds,
but first I must finish this childish contest
where one must stare the other out, not look
away, like a painting in a gallery, where
only the blink of an eye might restart time.

FINISTERRE

Nothing to do in this place
but turn and return, or stop
and look out into nothing;
ocean and sky in a blue
confusion, the curved shriek
of a gull.

Nothing to catch
the wind but a tourist's hair,
her summer linens blown,
her palm to the granite
cross, a squint smile
for a husband's camera flash.

*

Sun, after days of loose
Galician rain, is siphoning
moisture from the stone
of the afternoon, while shadows
creep by increments
from under the flowers,
their little hoods and bells
frail, incongruous in the rocks.

*

Just visible, at the foot
of the cliffs, a tiny vessel,
stopped, at anchor; a thin
figure lowering lines
and basket traps to the depths.

The great lamp sleeps my heart
my heart is contracting
after light. Aloneness
is the word I was looking for.

WHERE ARE YOU?

I'd guess
in a supermarket,
from the backing track of barcode bleeps
and the jerk-squeaky wheel
of a trolley, audible
on the phone.

At a distance, a child
bawls, its open mouth a black
hole into which the earth itself
might fall.

You speak in a confidential tone,
moving through the aisles,
your eye selecting
certain items.

*

You ring me back
from the car park, sitting
in your window-bubble.
In the boot, plastic bags settle
with a faint crackle.

The denizens of outer space
float about their business
or slowly drift away.

Earthbound,
I'm losing you.
There's not the reach on the line.
Somewhere in the universe
your voice is breaking up again.

WHEN I LAND IN NORTHERN IRELAND

When I land in Northern Ireland I long for cigarettes,
for the blue plume of smoke hitting the lung with a thud and, God,
the quickening blood as the stream administers the nicotine.
Stratus shadows darkening the crops
when coming in to land,
coming in to land.

What's your poison?
A question in a bar
draws me down through a tunnel of years
to a time preserved in a cube of fumes, the seventies-yellowing
walls of remembrance; everyone smokes and talks about the land,
the talk about the land, our spoiled inheritance.

SIN MÚSICA

The words cover more than they reveal.
I lift these lines from your virtual letter.

How short they fall
of real meaning. Your actual

touch was so much better
than words. I cover more than I reveal,

I know, but you were clear and cool
as air, and love a catar-

act or waterfall
into real meaning, simple

truth I fail to utter
in words that cover more than they reveal;

or the lifeless font of electronic mail,
here, at the point where it does not matter

how short they fall
of real meaning. Habitual,

I rearrange this useless clutter
of words, words;

words that cover more than they reveal.
How short they fall.

THE POETRY BUG

is a moon-pale, lumpish creature
parcelled in translucent skin
papery as filo pastry
patterned faint as a fingerprint
is quite without face or feature
ear or eye or snout
has eight root-like
tentacles or feelers, rough
like knuckly tusks of ginger
clustered at the front.

Invisible to the naked eye
monstrous in microscopy
it loves the lovers' bed or couch
pillow, quilt or duvet
and feeds, *thrives* I should say
on human scurf and dander
indeed, is never happier
than feasting on the dust
of love's shucked husk
the micro-detritus of us.

BOREDOOM

We nursed the wounded gull to death
in the end, attended its small funeral, as the rain
beat down on the shed's tin roof. Tightrope-walked

on the high back walls, took giant steps, ran errands,
Milk, Potatoes, Silk Cut, Special Mince. We swung
in arcs on a length of flex from a lamppost,

racing our own shadows. Shot at aliens
dancing on a screen, pushing coin after coin
in the slot: reached level five, the mother ship.

The world was due to end next week
according to someone whose brother had read
Nostradamus. *Magpies, two for joy. Walk round ladders, quick,*

touch wood. We mimed the prayer of the Green Cross Code
and waited, good, at the side of the road.
Blessed ourselves when the ambulance sailed

by on a blue (our fingers, toes). Lay awake
in the fret of the night, thinking about the Secret
of Fatima, the four-minute warning, the soft-boiled egg.

Our boomerang did not come back. Frisbees
lodged in the canopies of trees forever, turning black.
I poked out moss from paving slabs, half-dreamingly,

with an ice-pop stick, then leapt at the looped rope
of my name called from a yard, and dawdled home,
trailing a strange tune on the xylophone railings.

The future lived in the crystal ball
of a snake preserved in alcohol in my grandmother's attic.
I looked, on tiptoe, out through the lens

of the highest window; learned the silver river's turn,
the slogans daubed on the ancient walls,
the column of smoke where something always burned.

JEAN

Because last night and because today,
you fix a drink to steady the shakes.

The soft cottage walls are swelling
into your cells, spores falling,

freely, into the pit of tomorrow,
flammable, this life, this sorrow:

fountain pen; an old picture
in a cardboard frame, the face a crater.

Here's to the cruellest joke, Jean,
that it came too late, and never.

Justin Quinn

By way of background, what is the earliest poem in this selection? 'Terrorism'? Can you remember when and where it was written, and in what spirit? More particularly, what do you recall of Ireland and its poetry at the moment of composition, and of how you defined your creative ambitions starting out?

Yes, this was my first published poem, and also a kind of public coming out as a poet. Up to this my work at poetry, and ambitions for it, were completely in the closet, as I was growing up in South Dublin, going to a school that took no interest in the arts, beyond a Gilbert and Sullivan production at Christmas. So there was really no point in talking much about this stuff with peers. I mean, friends knew I spent my free days trawling the second-hand book shops like Webbs on the quays, etc., and would return with battered old Penguin editions, but it wasn't something that impinged on our conversation, rather as if one had a friend whose sexual fetish you found so embarrassing you couldn't mention it in conversation. I was lucky enough that John Banville took the poem for The Irish Times, and then everyone knew.

It was a shock also when everyone, mostly, said they couldn't understand it. I can't really say what came first: the title or the poem, but I do know that I wanted a political glint to a description of what seemed to be a personal anecdote.

As for Ireland's poetry at the time, the great generation of Heaney, Longley and Mahon circulated above us at a great height, and in between there was little that attracted me. Hartnett was fascinating to encounter, Durcan's poetry meant an awful lot to me in my early twenties, for political reasons.

For myself, I had no real ambitions beyond trying to write decent poems. I didn't have a project. Later when David Wheatley, Bill Mc-

Cormack and myself founded Metre, it came out of frustration (at least for David and myself) with how boring and in-bred Irish poetry publishing was. Very few forthright reviews, very little sustained interest in what was going on beyond the borders of the country.

Many of the early poems in The 'O'o'a'a' Bird consider bloody history beneath the surface of the city you grew up in, Dublin, yet you were already living in Prague by the time it came out. Was that historical awareness something you always had or something that became more pronounced living in Prague? Evidence of more recent political upheaval must have been still very much on the surface when you arrived there.

The interest pre-dated my first visit to Prague, in early 1992. The upheavals in Prague were of a different variety—virtually bloodless, but there was a huge shift in consciousness after the departure of communism. It was strange to be here at that time, when there were so many expectations about the West, which the Czechs wanted to join, once again. One was constantly caught in large historical issues, even in the most banal of conversations and social situations.

Did this sense of inhabiting two republics at once, and perhaps being always somewhere between them, feed into the liminal feel of much of the 'Days of the New Republic' sequence and subsequent work? Weekends, suburbs, waking ... In 'Sundays' it is 'events off-stage / [That] fade toward other lives', and in 'Geography' a river enters the sea 'like mountain soup / Into the largesse of salt water.'

I remember the poems were written very fast, mainly in Dublin, where I was working on my PhD and also doing a lot of work as a waiter. I was also drifting in and out of the creative writing seminars of Trinity, with Michael Longley and Peter Fallon. I remember that it was liberating to have another place, a home from home outside Ireland, to go to for a month or more at a time, though I still very much thought of myself as a resident in Ireland.

What attracted you about the second person, and the imperatives? Is it meant to seem less personal? Were there any particular poems that acted as models for that point of view?

I imagine that in part I was tired with the prevalence of the first-person singular in poetry both at home and abroad. The thrilling little epiphany of the personal, as somebody looks out the window at the sunset and realises that, well . . . it's never that they have to take the dog out for a walk, but something much more profound. Great poems can be written in this mode, but the proliferation of awful ones in this style probably pushed me in the opposite direction. That is, as some God-like person tells the writer or reader, for that matter, what's going on. I liked the ambiguity of voice—it wasn't clear, or shouldn't have been, if it's the poet talking to himself in the second-person singular or some outside agency, or the poet talking to the reader. It's also a mode that is fairly firmly rooted in regular conversational modes (unlike, weirdly, the first-person singular epiphany monolog).

When Robert Potts reviewed the book in *Poetry Review*, he said that it seemed very distant and impersonal, and he's not a critic who pines for the confessional mode, and he's also someone who's opinion I take seriously. I spent a lot of time thinking about this while writing the poems of my second book.

As for models, I can't remember any though I did like the idea of rewriting other poems—by Pasternak, John Ash. I also wove quotations and attitudes from a wide range of other writers into the weave of the poems—Jefferson, Yeats, Jerome McGann, Hélène Cixous, Eavan Boland, Joyce. One poem was supposed to feel like an outake from

Colm Tóibín's *The Heather Blazing*. Another drew on the deathless film *Who Framed Roger Rabbit?* I've always been entranced by Benjamin's idea of writing a book that entirely consisted of quotations. Recycling is as good for literature as it is for the environment.

Your second collection, Privacy, *is arguably your most formal book. Here we have the villanelle of 'A Strand of Hair', for example, or the Italian sonnet of 'Highlights'. Did these forms happen organically, or we they part of a formalist conviction? How absolute was/is your determination to stanza and rhyme?*

Organic or conviction. That's a tough one. For the previous fifteen years I had practiced conventional forms so that they were an organic conviction. For me this question doesn't really apply to any art. Take a dancer for instance: one doesn't ask a dancer if he's able to do what he does organically, spontaneously. Or a painter. Artists and writers can reach a point where they wield the hard-won techniques naturally, like a dancer. The form becomes a mode of thought, not a mould for it. A way of measuring breath and cadence. Which is a way of life, and a trajectory of emotion and sensibility.

What has changed over the years however is my attitude to the tradition of half-rhyme that you and I both began with, inherited from Mahon, primarily, I think (at least in my case). I've moved away from this in recent years, towards an older practice of full rhyme, which many 20th century poets in English felt was too restrictive. The notional school of poetics that we both attended taught us to hide our louche rhymes in complex stanzas with a natural speaking voice. I still remain committed to the last two, but really don't see any point in half-rhyme any more: either rhyme it or don't. It's a non-effect, in aural terms. Much better to explore other formal possibilities in the manner of Graham or Ammons or Ginsberg, to name just three of my favourites.

I've noticed this, how the rhymes have become fuller. The argument in defence of half-rhyme is that it broadens the palette of an otherwise rhyme-impoverished language. In 'Ukrainian Construction Workers' there is the wonderful rhyme of Moscow/Tesco. Surely the half-rhyme creates a lovely irony that wouldn't be available in full rhyme? Do you read these now and wince?

I think rhyme should be a way of thinking, a way of constructing an argument, of setting up contrasts that can't be got at through normal statements. It's one of the fundamental advantages poetry has over other discourses. Those ironies are just as available in full rhyme, only one has to work harder for them—to maintain natural speech patterns, with certain elements emphasized. Also I wonder about the effectiveness of sweet ironies that ultimately fly under the reader's radar. They might eventually be appreciated by the academic exegete of the IA Richards school, but what good is that to anyone? As a graduate of that school I thought that the ultimate attention to poetry was of that variety—the kind of the thing that critics like Christopher Ricks and Helen Vendler do so brilliantly. But I've stopped believing in that. I think poetry should be attended to, and has historically been attended to, in a much cruder, rougher way, by people who aren't professionally employed to note those lovely ironies. Increasingly, the poetry I enjoy reading does that, like say the Cavalier poets, or Dryden, or Gunn. Their rhymes are full (or most of the time in Gunn), and sometimes they are full merely for phonetic effect, but that's OK too.

Isn't there a danger of fetishizing rhyme? Reviewers seem to work on a tacit principle that all rhyme is inherently worthy. Isn't there lots of crap rhyme about? What would strike you as examples of good and bad rhyme?

I dislike most of the rhymed poetry being written at the moment. Mainly because it's so awkward. If you look at the translation of the

Metamorphoses that Dryden edited and contributed to, you see a handling of rhyme by basically third-rate poets which is extremely competent. So I would agree with you that people are in general ready to slap the poet on the back for rhyming cat and mat. I think New Formalism in the US resulted in so many terrible poems, but I suppose if New Formalism hadn't arrived with its tedious manifestoes, then those poems would merely have been awful free-verse poems. I love the varieties of rhyme available nevertheless. I love the slapdash rhymes of Hacker, which can only be read at speed. I love the devious rhymes of Muldoon, in which all the text lying west of the right-hand margin seems merely there to accommodate the rhymes. Closest to my heart at the moment are the rhymes of Wilbur, especially in his later work. Occasionally throughout his oeuvre it seems that the rhymes are there merely as technical performance, at which point I'm roundly bored. But say in a recent poem like 'The House', they are completely at the service of beautiful speech and overwhelming emotion. Wilbur might seem *sui generis*, but that's only because he's one of the last ambassadors of the Cavalier style, like the last of the Gaelic bards.

Since you have mentioned him more than once, now would seem like a good moment for us to acknowledge the absolute centrality of Mahon's work and example to our generation. We were all in love with him! Do you agree that his influence, more than any other, created space for our generation?

Oh he was the man. I first read *The Hunt by Night* because nothing else was on the shelves in the early 1990s. When I launched my first book he was in the audience, with a copy of the book in his hands, checking the poems against the performance, and I was up there thinking, 'Oh Christ.' I remember reading an interview with him in the early 1990s where he complained that no-one was imitating him, and yet all us epigones were just about to jump out in the two or three years after. I think his type of poem—not Heaney's, not Longley's, not Boland's—is the one we all began to try to write. But his type of poem, and the way he wielded it, wasn't *sui generis* in its turn, but had a distinguished lineage from Auden, MacNeice (Auden before MacNeice, I think, despite all the talk, including Mahon's own), and Wilbur, and a host of others. It was also so marvellously unrural, and if you were a city boy like me, it was a relief to encounter that in Ireland. It was also a relief to read something that didn't obsess about Irish history and nationhood.

The blind alley, however, in Mahon's example was the irony and pathos. So much of what he writes, even at his best, is lament—for the lost peoples, for some pre-modern age. It was difficult to talk about anything in that Mahon poem without being ironically *sad* that one was living now, and not some other time. I kept running up against this in the late 90s in the poems I was writing—as I'd get towards the end of them they would start pushing me towards this ironic, sophisticated, punning sadness, no matter how much I kicked and struggled.

Is it too simplistic to read Irish history into your versions of Prague? It is hard to resist hearing Irish/English tensions in the uneasy Czech/Soviet history of 'Ukrainian Construction Workers'. 'You meet them . . .' (which, if I'm not mistaken, originally appeared as 'The Old Communists') seems to echo Yeats's 'Easter 1916' deliberately. It's a terrific poem, but an angry one too.

I wrote those things in direct response to my experiences here, not as some kind of allegory of Ireland. But my homeland, and the poetic tradition of English has shaped me and made me alert to certain things and not to others. Several Czech friends have remarked that no Czech poet has written a similar poem about the old communists that one still bumps into here and there. I didn't have Yeats in my head when I wrote the first lines of the poem, and I only realized the echo afterwards, which I suppose is proof of the depth of the influence: it has changed from being influence to element that one breathes.

In the last two years or so, I've found myself writing poems about Ireland, both on the personal and political levels, which I more or less avoided for a decade, as I felt I somehow had no purchase on the place anymore. But for various reasons I've been spending longer periods in the Old Country again, utterly fascinated by the changes that have taken place. And that has given me a theme: comparison of historical periods, to put it as sexily as possible. That is, when I grew up there and what it's like now.

Yeats's presence appears to have become more central to your private imagination. Is this true? Do you think it's more possible now, for poets of our generation, to use Yeats's influence without it proving too great an anxiety?

Occasionally I teach a semester-long course in Prague devoted entirely to his poetry. I've been doing that for about the last decade. The labyrinth of his thought and imagination is all-engulfing, and I find myself illustrating many points in conversations with anecdotes from Yeats's life, as well as his epigrams; and all the while the soundtrack of his poetry is playing in my head. I don't think it's because I'm Irish that he appears to be the supreme poet in English of the past few centuries. As for the anxiety, I can't say I feel that: there's just the sheer pleasure of his work, the originality (and occasional craziness) of his thought, his utter allergy to platitude. I remain mesmerized by the long sequences of The Tower for the way they integrate traditional lyrics into large intellectual structures in a way, to my mind, that hadn't been done before.

That idea of using traditional lyrics in large intellectual framework seems to explain the scope of the sequence that forms almost all of Fuselage.

That's what I was trying to do there. I suppose I was also thinking of fuselage as a kind of sleeve of phenomena, much like the shadow in Plato's cave, and trying to describe that sense of being surrounded by, and part of, that. Again, it's almost ten years ago since I wrote it, and I find it difficult to get back to what was going on then. When I look at it now I mainly see all the borrowings—from Whitman, Jorie Graham, Eliot, Don DeLillo, Ammons. I needed the help of all those poets to make forays out of the traditional forms I'd be working with almost exclusively up to this.

'I Wake Early ...' first appears in the sequence at the core of Fuselage, and then as a stand-alone poem in your very next book, Waves & Trees, with apparently only one very small revision. Can I ask you about the rationale behind this?

As I mentioned before, recycling is good for poems. Moreover, within that poem itself, I've recycled one stanza of Paul Valéry's 'Palme'. It's a very loose version, and my way of acknowledging how important the French poet was to me at the time. I wrote this poem on the cusp of finishing *Fuselage* and beginning the poems of *Waves & Trees*, and after that immediately I wrote 'Fury', which opens the latter book. So the inclusion in *Waves & Trees* has more to do with my own uncertainty about where one collection ends and the next begins. Because of the way it involves mythology in an understanding of the land, it belongs in *Fuselage*, but for the way it depicts Central Europe, I felt it was natural to include it in *Waves & Trees*.

Both Fuselage and Waves & Trees begin with big poems, seeming to try to reconcile history and the individual. Does the composition process of a poem like 'Fury' differ from shorter pieces? Do you set out to write a big one, or does that just happen? More generally, how do you write poems?

It's fairly different, primarily because composing a long poem stretches out over a longer period. 'Fury' was intended from the outset to be a Pindaric ode, in the style of Dryden, so I knew that each part had to be heterometrically different, down the last gallop of trimeters in the final part. Short poems of a page or two usually take one or maximum two mornings, though 'January First' took 18 months. So yes, I usually set out to write longer ones, as I have a sense that possibilities will open up in certain directions if I can get the tone and form correct. As for writing poems, a typical example for me would be a sonnet. That can take from 20 minutes to 4 hours, which is then followed by polishing. I go running around the apartment looking at dictionaries, Wikipedia, looking out the window for a few seconds, checking email and Facebook. I like these distractions, as they usually delay the momentum and make me aware of other possibilities in the poem. One of the issues I have to deal with is that very momentum, which sometimes pushes me to finish poems too tritely.

Light is very important in your poems. 'January First', 'Even Song', and 'Affair' seem bathed in various lights and shades. What does light represent in your work? That's a daft way of coming at it! Let me rephrase it: what is it about evening and its light that makes for poems?

I'm tempted to answer facetiously and say it represents light. I think that such basic physical aspects of existence such as light, the weather, the seasons, vegetation don't really represent things in poetry or literature; rather all the complications and machinery of literature are merely there to intensify our awareness of these fundamental phenomena. Most poems begin out of simple impulses like: 'isn't that light fantastic?', 'isn't that man/woman beautiful?', 'isn't it awful that person is dead?' The three poems you mention are about, respectively, being burdened with a child, nostalgia for one's home country, and imagining having an affair with one's wife; but really you could argue that those themes are just decorations on the fundamentals such as changing light, seasons, vegetations—the poems live for those things and *not* vice versa. Stevens has a beautiful epigraph to one poem, from Mario Rossi: 'the great interests of man: air and light, the joy of having a body, the voluptuousness of looking.' Everything else is secondary.

Evening's good because it's an in-between stage, when you can question the solidity of things. Daylight objects are still perceptible, but they're kind of floating off from their moorings ever so slightly. Maybe poetry, and art in general, needs to be reminded that things are malleable. But this isn't metaphorical, this doesn't represent anything else. The actual things are there and they actually seem less substantial.

Waves & Trees ends with a sequence of sixteen beautiful little 12-line poems. Though not set as a sequence, they nonetheless read as a piece. Do you intend your poems to be conversing with one another, or is that just inevitable in poems composed close together?

Sometimes I make them refer to one another, but also, I find they talk to each other even when my back is turned. One has the same preoccupations over time and that comes out not just in themes but also turns of phrase, etc. As for that particular run of poems, they were composed in one go over a month or so. I was interested in the compression of rhymed dimeter, as you push the rhymed right side up against the left margin. How much space does language need to say something? It was also done as a kind of a dare to my Czech translator, Tomáš Fürstenzeller: I said to him that poetry with those parameters couldn't be translated. I'm happy to say he proved me wrong. Furthermore on the idea of compression, I sometimes think long poems are amplifications of the possibilities implicit in short poems, so it's hard to say what is footnoting what.

In the newer poems from your fifth collection, Close Quarters, *like 'Seminar' and 'Russian Girl on Pařížská', your relationship with Prague seems both mediated and interrupted by other elements. These elements give both poems a lovely estrangement, as if the speaking self in the poems is or feels invisible. Do you feel more at home in Prague and Czech now, almost twenty years later, or less? More generally, do you see the city remaining your actual and imaginative home indefinitely?*

At home in Prague: I feel very at home here and would ultimately like my bones to rest in this land. I've a decent working relationship with the language, so perhaps that means that I no longer feel as though I have to confront the culture here and work it out. Now I experience other cultures *through* it. For instance, on the level of reading, I'll often read non-Anglophone novels or poetry in Czech translation first (especially the Russians and Poles, who are much better encountered in another Slavic language). The city has become a place for me to look at the world, whereas previously it was me looking at the city, working out what I think of it, etc. Three years back I wrote a long poem entitled 'Café Slavia' in which I used a venerable old café as exactly that type of vantage point, on that occasion to look at Ireland. Prague is a particularly good place to look at the world from, since it's been a cross-roads for most of the last millennium. It also balances between East and West in a precarious way, thus constantly precipitating questions about democracy, corruption and general civic values. These are good things for any artist, or citizen, to be thinking about.

Can you say something about the versions of love and desire that appear in 'Child', 'Divorce' and 'First Spring Days'? Every poet, it seems to me, has to find his or her own way of reconciling the life s/he lives with the one represented in the poems. How do you go about it?

I faced that difficulty at the launch of my first book in 1995, in which there was a poem entitled 'Masturbation Sonnet with Viburnum Blossom'. I was standing near the top of the room in Bewley's with my publisher at the time, the ever amiable and amazing Michael Schmidt, watching my aunts and friends of parents filing in. He nudged me mischievously and said, 'Go on, read the sonnet'.

More generally I often find myself saying things in poems about my life, etc., that I would find impossible to say in person, or in an update, and I say this while deploring the Confessional School. Some of the poems in Close Quarters are about trouble in a marriage—some of it's autobiographical, some of it isn't. 'Divorce' was written as a love poem, and the title came afterwards as I was thinking about good friends of ours who were in the process of getting divorced. I was thinking of the ways in which love can flip over like that (and sometimes back again).

The one uncollected poem here, 'Nostalgia', describes post-boom Ireland. What's the poem nostalgic for: the boom, or the pre-boom years of your early adulthood in Dublin, or that youthful clarity of vision that sees each thing as itself and its own purest metaphor?

The title is partly ironic. Etymologically it means 'the longing for the journey home'. It's just nostalgic about a place that is layered over with ghosts. I'm not nostalgic in the least—and I hope the poem doesn't express this—for youthful clarity of vision. I go back to Ireland and I see the place through the 1980s, when I grew up there. One feels a greater connection with a place if, in Larkin's line, 'only that so many dead lie around', and you've known those particular dead. The poem is also a version of Frost's 'lover's quarrel with the world'—it's my lover's quarrel with Ireland. Don't think I care enough to write a nice poem for you. But obviously I care enough to write a poem.

TERRORISM

I would blame no bird,
When the slightest twig is snapped,
For its nervousness.
Suspended above it all,
Held by steel and brick,
We live inside their silence,
Years after such acts.

from DAYS OF THE NEW REPUBLIC

I. SUNDAYS

You lie in through their quiet mornings,
The only things awake for miles
Being birds, leaves shivering into wings,
And trees that when the sky exhales
Sway back and forth like tremor gaugings.

Different cars in every driveway
Wait stockstill on your neighbours
To be unlocked, ignited by
A key and driven down for papers,
Or to stand in carparks above the bay.

And in the city's peace, the news-
Papers' drama, page after page

Of trouble, seems bizarre, confuses
The calmness. Like events off-stage
They fade toward other lives & lose

Whatever force they had beside
These self-effacing homes and lawns.
Nothing, no-one bats an eyelid.
Three doors down somebody yawns
And suddenly pulls the curtains wide.

XX. GEOGRAPHY

Start with the nothing-could-be-simpler
Line where skies depend on seas,
Endless talks on talks, palabra
Of reflections and replies
To what winds howl and rainstorms jabber.

Then move in toward the bay, forever
Just about to close its grasp
Around a lake, the green drugged river
Seeping out like mountain soup
Into the largesse of saltwater.

It's all around you now, its growth,
Its thru-ways, hoardings, open shops,
Its people crowding every width
Of pavement, cranes above the rooftops,
Mayoral, watching life beneath.

And then the suburbs. You're there somewhere
On some road, ridiculously named,
Living at a certain number,
Waking up from rooms you dreamt
To where you gradually remember.

LANDSCAPE BY BUS

Look out the window—half
A landscape, half its trees.
Switch focus. Reflections of
The rest float by on these.

At sixty miles an hour
The world's being folded back
Into a suitcase. Where
Oh where will I unpack?

A STRAND OF HAIR

I never asked you for your hand,
Or in some man-to-man talk asked your father.
So light will be our wedding-band.

The other day I found an errant strand
Of your dark hair and held it, like a tether,
And though I never asked you for your hand,

We will be married, and
As this, hardly to be felt, twines round my finger,
So light will be our wedding-band.

So light that five years hence who could demand
Their freedom? From what, tied like this? Neither
Asked the other for their hand—

One London summer's morning it just happened.
The sun's rays wound gold heat about us there.
So light then was our wedding-band.

And you won't ask me to leave my rain-cursed land
Forever for your city with its saner weather.
I'll never ask you too. Give me your hand.
So light will be our wedding-band.

SPYHOLE

My eyeball grooved into this hemisphere,
This stud of solid glass, I see the world
Beyond the door of our apartment swirled
Into strange shapes, as unreal as they're clear:

The white-walled corridor, fluorescent lights,
The other doors that wait there for an opening,
All comically bent round my eye, all sloping
Under duress in the lens's sights.

I lift my head away and suddenly
Things have the look of truth again: the chairs
Don't curl around my gaze, the table bears
Its load of fruit and papers steadily,

The walls keep floor from ceiling, perfectly flat
And upright. Unlike the curved grotesquerie
Kept safely outside under lock and key,
This is real. This is where we're at.

Or rather, I am, at the moment. You're
Beneath the city on the Metro home,
Making the transfers, straphanging to the hum
And racket of each subterranean contour.

I shadow you the last stretch, leaving the wagon,
Then up and past the upright ticket stocks
Into the night, between the dreaming towerblocks
To where you reach home and are real again.

HIGHLIGHTS

Last night the couple in the flat above us
Were in full flight: tirades and injured feelings
Swung back and forth for hours across the ceiling
Like bad jazz solos, long and repetitious.
Last week we caught crescendos from Sibelius.
And now tonight around eleven stealing

Through carpets and concrete slabs a wild, freewheeling
Moan of utter joy, which is their Anschluss.

But otherwise we'd never know they're there
And easily forget their sixth-floor sitcom.
We get on with our own lives—work and leisure,
Chores tending to our household appliances—
Which seem the same as theirs (the noise, the rhythm)
Apart from what goes on between, in silence.

BACKGROUNDS

1. POLITICAL

It is 19—.
X years have passed
Since the upheavals.
Everything must be placed
Against that background.

2. AESTHETIC

I placed a jar in Milíčov.
Unlike the nearby towerblocks it was round
And nothing much was within reach of
Its glassy empery.
I translate by profession
And have no time for trumpery:
In that age of grim oppression
It should have been the catalyst
Of change, but wasn't. It was a jar.

But then perhaps the most acute of analysts
Could have isolated the microscopic gyre
Set going somewhere on that afternoon
And Y years later stormed the parliament.

3. PERSONAL

It was near the end of June,
One of those really warm evenings, the windows of the apartment
Opened wide, summer insects gliding in and out
Trafficking in small amounts of food and blood.
Thirty degrees centigrade or thereabouts.
Occasionally, the long muslin curtains lifted up and billowed.
Alex, Élisabeth and Eamon were sitting at our table.
We had just finished dinner. L'Orfeo
Was playing on CD (highlights, the Opera Collection label).
I went to make the coffee.
Alex was telling us about the Nixon years,
The huge complexity, the way the scandals blossomed in the public eye,
The chiaroscuro of the unknown and the known, the bright careers
Destroyed, the President believing his own lies.
From the kitchen, it seemed that Alex had constructed a maquette
Of Washington with all its shady machinations, and this
Now floated just above the table, our eyes on it,
Believable down to the last acanthus.
Each further word and phrase
Had the effect of altering it however slightly—
New colours and textures moved across its surface
As he went on explaining quietly.
Somehow Orpheus and Charon were a part of this—
The tendrils of his clauses stretching out in all directions

Kept twining themselves round the trills and dour cadenzas
Expressed into the apartment's air by Japanese electronics.
Somehow the colours of our walls were part of this as well,
The arrangement of the furniture,
The way the others sat there all the while,
The way that I, amidst the after-dinner clutter,
Was simply standing in the kitchen, thinking.
I placed the mocha on the hob and waited in the background.

UKRAINIAN CONSTRUCTION WORKERS

They travel maybe two days on a bus
              And end up here
On pittance, no insurance, bread and beer—
The paperwork looked after by their boss,

Which means that they're accounted for as goods.
              They don't exist.
If they fall off a ledge they won't be missed.
Nobody will be buried in the woods.

The street is quiet. A cloudy, wintery murk.
              At 9 a.m.
Already they've got four hard hours behind them.
They drain their beers and go back to the falsework.

Two Czechs walk by. One says, 'At least this time
              They're not in tanks.'
These days they're here to walk the scaffolding's planks
And build not blast a city in its prime—

Whichever it is is much the same to them.
                    The joists, the blocks
Swung into place to found a bank or box
Five hundred lives inside (by rule of thumb),

These things are plywood-light to their strong hands.
                    Their alien eyes
See straight through solid concrete to the skies
Because they know not one naïve brick stands

A chance in hell against the whim of Moscow.
                    Transparent things
Like these estates of towerblocks, civic buildings,
The new life promised everyone by Tesco,

Are what transparent men construct and tear
                    Straight down tomorrow.
What's left is less a capital and more a
Million people moving in the air.

PRAGUE, 1996

■ ■ ■

You meet them at mid-afternoon receptions
where they have come from their small offices
in ministries. They smile and they profess
an interest in the IMF and options,

anxious to present the facts they know,
yet curious if they feel that you know more,

as if the market and the trading-floor
had been invented just two months ago.

Their ties: diagonals of blue and white
designed a year after the tanks came in,
a sense of speed imparted by flecks of brown;
their shirts the colour of collective wheat;

their smiling tolerance of the dissidents
who now hold power, like parents who indulge
idealistic children and won't divulge
hard truths just yet, their sympathy immense;

their bonhomie; their polished anecdotes—
all this suggests you couldn't have them shot
and afterwards feel good about it, not
because you like the golden Jakeš quotes

(you do) but because they impersonate
a human being oh so well; will even
take out photographs of faded children
(who seem improbable in build and trait).

What they won't mention: X years back the period
when in the role of high apparachiks
they suddenly found that three or so rough weeks
and their Socialist Republic had disappeared,

much as when in a crowded tram you find
your wallet gone, the banknotes and IDs
spirited away by murderers and thieves,
and other dirty bastards of that kind.

■ ■ ■

Observe the sky: it changes
and remains the same. Cope
of cloud manoeuvres, flow
and fusillades of rain.
You fall up through it

endlessly, you never
come upon its edge.
Its flame is various,
is light and luxury
one moment, then sheers off

and leaves the streets and houses
closed and utterly bereft,
their people sunk back down.
Junkies veer and drift
through the concourse of the Metro.

Lodged inside their skulls
are jewels of *Jetztzeit*. Expanse
of joy and mainly power,
'vital, consecrating, celestial,
all things dissolved into

the waves and surges of
an ocean of light'. The world
is spinning fuselage
& swerves & bends & swoops
in answer to our will

though we don't see or know
each other, what spirit
each is of. We flame forth
beautifully, apart;
shimmer, slide and flow.

■ ■ ■

Flashes, specks: if not men and women crowding fast in the streets
what are they?

They flange out far across the special zones, scud
the pavements' edges,

surge and tack this way and that, into the main drag
or trickle through the sidestreets, saunter,

build up and then the sign, spick torrent flowing loose
across the path of columns of stalled cars:

to the sky-hooked eye an immense panorama
of fluidity and ochlocracy—

mostly hair and flurried cloth—which prompts the voice-over to say
fabric

(feel the gear-change, the summoned boost,
like a powerful elevator accelerating upwards into

explanation, overview, expanse,
electronic overlay of appropriate statistics,

the pitch, the soothing timbre
assembled by men and women in dark rooms checking levels, watching
    monitors)

of society,
flesh made spectral,

sorted into a flaring, phosphorescing play
of flindered surface.

& I move through this:
air dense with overview and welded into place

by ampersands and copulae,
which reach and hook into the fabric

cladding me
(GAP jeans, NEXT sale shirt,

their 'Made in' tags discreet
white stigmas stitched on inside seams—

China, Indonesia—flashpoints, joint trade,
flouting of . . .

4402 6028 127* ****
the numbers wielded for the purchase,

connecting with the barcodes,
the tiny fibres

furiously knitting me into the flows, the circuits, the systems
as data: nondescript low buildings

bevelled gently into a hillside in Vermont or Meath,
which house

a layered hum of cooling fans and airconditioning,
& a mainframe, hold it in the undulant landscape,

its dreaming, its sleepless sorting of
the figures coming in from Europe and East Asia)

& make
a massive rippling arras of the world,

of these streets crowded fast:
buoyancy, lift

myriad shuttling motions,
billowing array of coloured stitchwork. Facets

glint here, are grazed matt there, but largely
shimmer, slide and flow.

■ ■ ■

Which get the go-by from the Thames.
Southwark, Waterloo—the streets
deserted by their week-day temps,
the multinational ziggurats

slumbering lightly, and Starbucks shut.
The beautiful designs abut
the deeper blacks and blitzkrieged browns
of some place local. An old lush clowns
at the bar of our Holiday Inn,
then comes up to us, flicking her hair:
'I hate you tourists . . . I live here.
Just fuck off home.' Which is Dublin
for Jack, Stockholm Shane, and Prague
myself. Two days and no jet-lag.

■ ■ ■

They are for commerce and they hold out sex
and bread, apartments, videos, meat,
street after street
across the valley-floor for all our sakes.

Billboards stand forth
from roadsides and the gables of large buildings
suggesting how our flesh and blood can fill things
and can fuck things, and all they can't afford.

The river gleams
and winds its way through these diverse arrangements
beneath the cloudless heavens—strange, immense;
and the houses come forth in the sun's good beams.

The day unfolds
and I explain what I know to my son.
Newsprint is swirled and swept off at a run
along the path; the brown leaves move in shoals.

. . .

I wake early into
the already azure day.
The leaves, still sleeved in dew,
adjust themselves and sway
like tiny tremor-gaugings.
The black rampaging gangs
that flooded to-&-fro
throughout the night in dreams
(in time to passing trams)
linger briefly, then go.

Receding southwards, deep
into the continent,
a goods train threads one steep
green river valley bend
after another. Thunder
slow-fades to faint trundle.
The fields of yellow rape
stretch both ways from the river
to the interior;
they ripple and stand ripe.

Gaze folded into gaze,
flesh into flesh, like forests
risen in a maze.
The earth is widely forced
by myriad points of view.
So many—wakeful, new—

that flock and scintillate,
each with its glint of self,
plying its trade, its sylph
of silver concentrate.

The moving crowds are caught
by different tracts and cameras.
They wander into shot
and join the swelling arras
for a few moments when
they are the people, then
drift out of their bit parts
back into open day.
I spread my arms and pray.
I love how each day starts.

The roots of this tree stretch
to the entrails of the world
for its deep water; they fetch
it up into the curled
leaf waiting at the height
inside the sky's blue heat,
and for the heavy fruit—
stone folded in sweet flesh.
Eyes that see afresh,
in joy, have this dark root.

Set deep within the eye—
desire: its shuttles and warps
furiously multiply.

The overlapping orbs
load tales into the earth
of death and monstrous birth,
of pristine female beauty
relaxed and unconcerned
that all the world is burned
by some god for her body.

For mine. I stand in clay
and slowly I am covered
by my love's glint and play,
who once moved through the covert,
oblivious and free,
joy of a body, fear
of nothing, and first light
gathering everywhere,
before a sudden flare
of day-star. Then my flight.

for Petr Borkovec

FURY

I

High ceilings. People drifting through
or stopped in groups of two or three.
Outside is Sunday, slightly overcast
but there's a lightness filling up these rooms.
    Talk merges and moves through guest after guest.

It glides, it gets held up, it suddenly zooms
      in on deep feeling or
doesn't—merely skims and plays
      on surfaces—
elections, software, films, what chain store has what vase.
      A gargoyle emphasis,
   a histrionic roar.

II

Bodies hang down from this talk
  and bend and curl about the furniture.
      These girls of twenty-two
      were once glimpsed in a glade
      and a continent knew
      it had been born again.
      No lambency of Claude
      could catch the perfect grain
  of their new flesh, its force, its huge allure,
or how it draws up leaf and stalk.

III

      Our host is one who knows
a batch of languages and the ancients
      in the original,
is an original herself whose pose
      of pliant deference
sweetens a strength and stealth of mind, withal
      as simple as a rose,
her gathered beauty, her instinctive sense
      of what's hospitable.

And here's one who's just finished her first book,
    who gestures with bright speed,
whose eyes move over people with a glint
    of joy in how they look,
in how they move and talk, each turn and trait,
    her head gently inclined
into the rush and backwash of it, a hook
    that swims amidst the spate
and snags upon the whole of human kind.

    Another moving past
writes film reviews for a magazine
    that only wants the cleft
and face that suits in Hollywood have passed.
    Her mockery is keen,
herself a beauty unmatched by the weft
    of starlets in the cast.
A man might curl about the crust she's been
    just picking at and left.

IV
    Perspiring and confused,
  I wake up at a dark small hour,
    it all unloosed.
Outside the silence sanded by a shower.
    Without the sun,
  I can't tell day-events from dreams.
  They merge and phosphoresce as one
    across the screen.
Bricks and flesh and sky slide into streams

of changing figures.
Then emptiness. No one, nothing flickers.
Not an eyelid or a lip. Not a word.
    The earth will be wiped clean
    of these girls moving round—
        they will ungird
their limbs and melt back in the ground.

V

The Furies come and go
adding to their huge ruck:
some thirty years ago
a woman drove a truck
up onto a dense pavement
and knocked eight people dead.
Before she swung in payment
a few years on, she said
the only sense of guilt
that lingered in her mind
was that she hadn't killed
much more of human kind.
I think of her pure eyes
flung headlong at high speed,
dismissing alibis,
adjournments, how we plead,
our interesting differences,
our spectacular bribes,
our loopholes and small clauses.
All this she simply wipes
from off the earth's round face—

would like to, anyway.
I move about the place,
around the rooms. I stay
in conversation with
other invented bodies
caught in codes and kith—
their fugal melodies.
First things go so far back,
if they go back at all.
A lengthy wandering tack
or simply one straight fall
led from them to palabras
that mirror and reply.
They show our different labours
and to the seeing eye
they show the whole world held
out in great space—a stone
that's endlessly compelled
to turn about the sun,
so rich with soil and root
that dream the years and days.
Much like a branch with fruit
held forth for us to praise.

JANUARY FIRST

Not a sound across the land
when I step off the shore
onto the frozen band
of the river clamped like ore.

A clean break. The light
is sharp and cold and new.
The houses dwindle from sight,
the cars are far and few.

And as I skate and veer
out to the small island,
saddled on my shoulders

riding the troughs and rollers
is a child, tiny and silent,
carried over from last year.

AFFAIR

Because I don't know your address
I can't just jump onto a tram
and ride across the city, trees
and streets going by as in a dream

until I get off at the stop
and nothing's moving in this heat.
The hill up to your block is steep
perhaps; lindens climb its height

or maybe beech or ash instead.
Plantains stud the pavement's grime,
that much is certain. The rest of it
keeps changing shape to fit the rhyme.

I stand upon the doorstep. I know
that you're somewhere inside the building
writing something or maybe now
just stacking up the dishes, biding

your time before I ring the bell,
well, well, although you didn't think
that I was on my way at all.
You ask me if I'd like a drink.

I don't know what we talk about.
And though it's later in the evening
when we lie down upon the bed
(which serves in daytime as divan)

the air is still quite hot outside.
Across the way, the ash or beech
or linden looms within the night.
Dead still. No breeze or other breach

of all this peace except our flesh
in movement for an hour or so,
us seamed against each other, flush
and happy. Then I get up to go.

But since I'm not sure if I've strayed
or been led back to those first days
when we two met and loved in a street,
in a block, in a room, in a bed like this,

it's hard to make my way home now,
and our two children, hand in hand,
wander the streets as they don't know
their own address or what has happened.

EVEN SONG

Blackrock or thereabouts.
The bay spreads, a colossal
riffled sheen of phosphor.
The sound of waves, faint shouts.

About five minutes ago
the tide was full and brimming.
It must be getting dimmer
gradually, but who'd know?

Clontarf supports the sky
like some great arm; it ushers
the early evening rush hour
hordes back home and dry.

Lights flicker on in Howth,
Baldoyle, and further suburbs
a good bit out from Dublin.
Steady colonial growth.

The odd container ship
sits fat on the horizon.
This light is mesmerizing.
The water meets the lip

of the observing eye
and shimmers in that opening,
loose flow of gold and opal
that grades into black lye:

it has a lift and sway
that makes the rest seem added,
even Howth, large shadows
of the groundswell's play.

I turn and find no land—
no town or station.
It has gone without saying,
and all that is to hand

is another mirroring sea,
which leaves me like a ripple,
a rift of mind that's slipped in
between a sea and sea.

HOTEL

*Let go. Be light
and float through here.*
Just overnight.
The sky so clear,

the sunrays gild
the room's décor.
Slowed now, stilled,
I am no more

than what connects
them and the TV's
smaller complex
lambencies.

PATIENCE

Game after game
I deal myself—
no hand the same—
and the hours dissolve.

King up, ace out,
gather and fold . . .
I am about
forty years old

or ten, wide-eyed.
I am my mother
or father. Outside
there is some weather.

SMALL FURY

The whole show folds:
the dog days go
and the land yields
to a sheath of snow.

Leaves sail and flare
away around
in chutes of air,
light on the ground,

wheeled furiously through
much larger turns
and smaller too
to brake and burn.

ELEGY

They go. You turn to say a word
or tell them a new joke, and they
    leave what you've said unheard.
        They've dropped away

into the dark that's everywhere
around us, sleeved so cleverly
    in sunlight, summer air,
        good company.

They go. After their earthly stint
these parents, lovers, sisters, brothers
    are nothing but the print
        they've left on others.

They can't or won't come back. They go,
and children want to find out who

was that. How did you know
each other. You

begin explaining, but quite soon
the kids go back to their affairs—
return to the cartoon
or run downstairs

and out to play ball on the road
or tag with all the other chancers,
and you're left with a load
of useless answers,

becoming chronicle and lore.
The weight of it. You know too much.
And the shades raven for
your merest touch.

SEMINAR

beginning with a half-line by Evan Rail

I carry America into these young heads,
at least some parts that haven't yet got there—
Hawthorne's Salem, Ellison's blacks and reds,
Bishop's lovely lines of late summer air.

The students take quick notes. They pause or dive
for dictionaries and laptops, or turn to ask

a friend as new words constantly arrive.
The more they do the more complex the task.

They smoothly move from serious to blasé
and back again. I love the way they sit
and use their bodies to nuance what they say.
I lean forward to catch the drift of it.

When it's ended they'll switch back to Czech,
put on their coats and bags, shift wood and chrome
and ready themselves for their daily trek
across a continent and ocean home.

RUSSIAN GIRL ON PAŘÍŽSKÁ

At twenty you hold this street's attention
better than the Bolshoi could—
the boots, the perfume, not to mention
the bling and ermine on your hood.

The way you walk is slash and burn.
Like understatement's now a crime.
You leave a wake of men who turn
to make sure they were right first time.

They're like small countries who betray
their old allegiances a while.
Bound over as your vassals, they
blame others when they go on trial.

You yawn, head for a brasserie—
all gold and mirrors, lit like Christmas—
and join the two men drinking tea,
dressed in black suits, who mean business.

DIVORCE

You sleep there underneath
four squares of blue, your clay
dilating as you breathe,
oblivious to the day.

Which is birdsong, the slight
sea-noise of cars below,
serrated insect flight,
a chainsaw on the go

within a wooded ghyll,
working its way through
part of our world. These fill
the azure over you.

In it are sheens that pass,
the fleetest silverings
of sylph and self in glass,
as well as shadowings

suggesting foreign steppes
through walls of brick and ply,
or just weird tiny depths
in details of the sky.

It's as if you're lying under
the surface of the water
as pictures join and sunder
of mother, wife and daughter.

When you wake up I see
the fathoms that you swam,
and your eyes ask of me
who on earth I am.

FIRST SPRING DAYS

Out walking with one child in a papoose,
the other by the hand, cool in a hood
and throwing questions and some mild abuse,
we came upon two lovers in the wood.

We slowed to give them time, as we'd reckoned
we couldn't turn. They rose, a little coy,
and as we passed our eyes locked for a second,
on either side of that explosive joy.

CHILD

You are of neither sex
and both, about age four:
for instance how you flex
your muscles as you stare

with dreams of mannish strength
through your hair's girlish length

and sweep it from your eyes
just as a woman would
before, to my surprise,
you land a sure and good
punch in my balls and say
that is the Batman way.

This forces out a 'Fuck'
from somewhere deep in me.
Today I'm out of luck:
you shouldn't hear or see
difficult things like that—
they don't apply just yet.

But when? When? Your mother
and I embrace you more
than we do one another.
You are now where we store
our fun and like a parable
we've lately turned to marble.

A fluid piece of flesh
you fly between the plinths
and daily to the crèche
along the path, our prince
or princess, full of beans,
beloved of kings and queens.

NOSTALGIA

Back in Dublin. Spring. The place has gone to hell.
Crawling on its hands and knees back to the eighties
when only a few good restaurants were doing well
and the rest of us were happy eating fries and praties.

Out in Dún Laoghaire, on the seafront, one of the best
is prepping lobster and frying prawns from Dublin Bay
for the happy ghost of Charles J Haughey and his guest.
The ghosts of waves crash on the coast all night and day.

Shades everywhere. Even the children aren't free
of likenesses that play through gestures, words and eyes,
themselves blind to the ghosts. For them the sea's the sea,
the waves the waves, the blue skies weirdly still blue skies.

John McAuliffe

What is the earliest poem in this selection? Can you remember when and where it was written, and in what spirit? What do you recall of Ireland and its poetry at the moment of composition, and of how you defined your creative ambitions starting out?

I don't remember writing 'Going Places' but I remember posting it to *Poetry Ireland Review* when I was a student in Galway, in 1996 or thereabouts. I remember sitting in a cafe on campus trying to figure out which of about eight halfway presentable poems to send there and which to *Cyphers*, which Eiléan Ní Chuilleanáin edited. I liked her poems and when she wrote me a useful note about the poems, that meant almost as much as getting a letter from *Poetry Ireland* to say 'Going Places' would be published.

I was doing an MA by research in the English Department at the time. There were decades of back issues of *Poetry* on the shelves and *The Hudson Review* and *The Southern Review*, *Stand*, the *TLS*, *Crane Bag* and a fair selection too of twentieth-century American and Irish books (I remember reading a lot of Lowell, Stevens, Ginsberg, Kinsella's *New Poems 1973* and Derek Mahon's *Selected*), so I was reading poems, and writing, covertly and in a sort of vacuum, even though Galway was a very lively town for poetry and music around then. When I started, the Waterboys had been based outside Galway for a few years and The Quays pub, where they used play sometimes, had a tin roof over most of it and buckets around the floor for the rain. A couple of years later, that whole derelict area was all cafes and nice pubs.

Over a few years, I saw Seamus Heaney, CK Williams, Derek Walcott, Robert Creeley, Allen Ginsberg read in Nun's Island or in the refurbished arts centre on Dominick Street, and I'd see them afterwards in the smoky bar at the Atlanta Hotel. The first reading I attended, though, was given by Sean Dunne, in the lobby of the university library. A few short years later I saw a note and a photo in the front window of Kenny's Bookshop on High St saying that he had died at the age of 39: poetry was a public art in Galway and, I suppose, that chimed with growing up in Listowel too, which had an unusual share of writers living and working in the town.

I wasn't so conscious of 'Irish' poetry then. Reading Kinsella sent me to the Cantos and Mahon was the source of rumours about Lowell and Wilbur and Stevens. Of the visitors I read a lot of Creeley and CK Williams. And I started going to a monthly workshop in the Bridge Mills, a café/language school by the Corrib in town, where I met Tom French and Rita Ann Higgins (who invited me along) and Anne Kennedy and Eva Bourke, and the social life around the workshops clued me in to a different set of ideas about poetry, and to what might be at stake. Rita Ann and Eva had a real political commitment, in their poems as well as in their way of living and involvement in Galway's political life. Tom and I read and talked about American and British poetry as much as Irish poetry, I'd say. We were interested in how poems might use traditional forms without sounding traditional, where *traditional* meant the sort of national poetry and fiction on the university syllabus. I was even more bored with the kind of west of Ireland shtick that got written about Galway and Kerry: so my ambition for the poems was to not do those things; 'Going Places' looks out the window and sees not the *scenery* but the wires crossing it and then dreams up something else, which was part of trying to see things and my relation to them without falling into a stock pattern.

Living there, seeing all of those international poets, must have fed into those many horizon that punctuate A Better Life. Can I ask you to talk a bit about the draw of elsewhere here? I'm thinking especially of poems like 'A Good Story', 'Africa', and 'Today's Imperative'.

I wrote those poems after we moved to a part of Cork called Jewtown. Those couple of years in Cork, I was teaching part-time at secondary schools and universities, always on the bus or train from one classroom to another. I felt like I lived elsewhere.

Cork's literary world was rundown but lively, Bradshaw Books and Tigh na Fili running readings and publishing competitions; the Munster Literature Centre getting into its stride with Mary Johnston and Patrick Galvin and then Pat Cotter. And the Cork poets were different to the Galway poets, fiercely insular: the pub readings and events featured the same crew who'd been doing it for decades with their own histories and settled arguments, upholders of the true faith.

I wanted to swing the poems away from local turf wars if that makes sense and find another 'horizon', to use your word, for the poems. 'A Good Story' and the Horace version both have in mind canons of pastoral poetry, and Irish poetry as a branch of pastoral: I wanted to set the poems at some kind of angle to that, not repeating or just reacting against it. 'A Good Story' has a couple of found voices in it, beginning with a bit from the Bible, then a couple of imagined speakers which draws from family lore, my mother's grandfather's service in the RIC and the Royal Hong Kong Constabulary: that story probably predisposed me to look out for mongrel versions of what an Irish poem might be. And I wanted the poem, the first poem in the first book, to tell a different kind of national story, while also having an ironic sense of its own fabrications (that it's a 'good *story*') across its five-bar stanzas.

The original Horace ode imagines a lot of different places and then decides his own Sabine farm is the best of the lot. I loved the speed with which his poems shifted tone and direction. In 'Today's Imperative', I replaced his tour of different places with a tour of contemporary poets' subjects, so the poem has a set of thumbnail sketches of other poets' work. The poem finishes, like Horace's, by trying to say that all this might be ok, but that poems can, should pierce or surprise, cut a reader to the quick before they do anything else.

'Africa' turns out to be a variation (another one!) on Patrick Kavanagh's 'Epic'. For me, Kavanagh's 'drills' and 'melodeons' were as exotic as Yeats's Byzantium or Stevens' 'tigers in red weather': what I loved was how these poets shifted around in their poems, then homed in on recognisable but unsettling returns to the known world. To a particular historical moment. Or to the place of writing or reading. It's an effect I like, and 'Africa' is a poem that uses its title to find an angle on the big evenings of a North Kerry summer: I was interested, like most poets, in setting up unexpected and unlikely relations between places.

'A Vision of Rahoon' seems to take its cue from Joyce's 'She weeps over Rahoon'. How conscious, again, are such remakes? Dillon Johnston has even argued that much of 20th century Irish poetry has taken its cue from Joyce's invention and pastiche rather than Yeats's grand style.

We end up in the same corners as Yeats and Joyce whether we like it or not, so yes that one *was* fairly conscious about Joyce: at the time of writing it Nora Barnacle's cottage was being restored, on Bowling Green, and I'd a friend who rented a flat at the top of a house on Nun's Island which had a fruit tree outside its back window. In the half-reality of literary study, I imagined that this was the same place that Joyce had imagined as the scene of Michael Furey's last song in 'The Dead'. To complicate things a little further, I'd also meant the poem as a gloss on, or response to, Mangan's 'Vision of Connaught in the Thirteenth Century': at the time Rahoon's tower block flats were being prepared for demolition, its existing tenants moved out, and the land sold on to private contractors who built new estates there, called 'Cnoc an Oir'—or 'Fort Lorenzo': Gaelic/Celtic nostalgia *and* Roman aspirations!—plenty to bring Joyce out in a hot flush. So, one part of writing that poem, yes, was trying to jigsaw different corners or arguments into place, putting up flags or signals which relate it to the kinds of other reading or experience you might expect your reader to know too. Flagging up Joyce, but not repeating him, though really thinking more about Mangan. And O'Malley Construction. And making my own soundworld out of that.

On Joyce, though I loved reading *Portrait* and *Ulysses*, it's *Dubliners* I return to and re-read still. It's so clinical and sure, and raging too, with its use of gritty detail, its undercutting of romantic images, and its careful use of symbol and repetition, its attention to local detail balanced by attention to the stories' larger shape or form. But to read his poems was equally revealing, because there he seems so stuck in outdated modes. In terms of 'invention and pastiche,' Yeats's inventiveness was, and is, more of a practical inspiration than Joyce's to me, especially in terms of how his poems remoulded poetic forms and rhythms. I think he is more significant and also more continuously influential, maybe, than Dillon Johnston's book suggests: what Dillon reads as 'Joycean' might be better read as a reaction against Yeats. Seamus Heaney in *Station Island*, Muldoon in 'Incantata', Thomas Kinsella in *Nightwalker*, are very clearly appealing to Joyce as a model, but their whole idea of invocation, of writing contrary but definitively Irish elegy—or writing poems which mix together the personal and the current historical moment, seem more Yeatsian to me.

That last line of 'A Vision of Rahoon' is like an effect from the sound archive. In 'A Better Life' the poems return again and again to sound and recording: whether it's listening to a CD of sounds in 'Effects', or 'wad[ing] into the river with the boom' in 'Action', or re-entering the orbit of Radio Kerry in 'Medium Wave'.

I like poems which work aloud as well as on the page; I like to sound out how a poem works as I'm writing. So those sounds come into the poems with that in mind. Eliot talks about the 'auditory imagination', how a poet should draw on speech, 'the sounds he has heard', to make his own 'melody'.

And that sense of how technology sculpts or pieces together sounds to create an impression of a natural and self-contained shape is analogous to writing and revising notes to make lines, or poems, or books. I was doing some work with Eamon Little who makes documentaries, but who was then compiling a big archive of interviews and recordings of writers and I'm sure that experience also fed into the poems.

I remember listening to Peadar O Riada's music then, or was that later: I loved anyway the way he integrated found and unlikely sounds into his music, the noise of children or a plane taking off moving in and out of more formal tunes: each of those poems has 'found' or over-heard elements in them, bits of other people's speech or vocabulary which gets transformed, or redirected, or opened up, by the situation or contexts of the poem, like the character who listens, on a walkman and obliviously mid-river, to a programme called 'The Open Mind'.

Between your first and second books, you settled with your family in Manchester. The book title Next Door *seems to refer to England's proximity to Ireland, as well as the idea of the neighbourhood. Did you have that in mind naming the book?*

We moved to London in June 2002, just before *A Better Life* came out. So, while I didn't have an initial plan or plot for Next Door, the literal break from an Irish to an English context obviously changed the material. After we moved to Manchester in August 2004 I suddenly saw the po-ems I'd finished in London *together* and it seemed fairly clear that I had a set of poems which were concerned with combining the two Irish and English settings. Yes I liked trying to reformulate the relation be-tween Ireland and England as neighbourly or adjacent, *next door*, rather than its being oppositional. So the title called attention to that, but I also wanted the title to refer to the family life which the poems draw on. Many of the poems use images from one of those contexts to think about the other, the poems about the children, say, are as likely to fea-ture various borders or flags as the ones about post-industrial English cities will feature children flexibly re-making that world.

As for the strangeness, I did want to decentre the poems, if that makes sense: 'There is no capital of the world', says Milosz, a line I bore in mind across the book. But I wanted the book's Irish poems to feel as full of strange detail as the England-set poems, like Han Shan turning up in Páirc Ui Chaoimh in 'Clouds', or those African evangelists appearing by the Feale in 'Town'. That placing of things side-by-side, unlike things, but without too much drama, as when you get the Irish seaside town and racecourse venue Tramore alongside the Jewish idea of *eruvs* and my local Manchester park, Fog Lane, in one sonnet.

As I was writing those poems, and as *Next Door* was taking shape, I also read my way into life in England: my friend Liam Harte was editing an anthology of Irish autobiographical writing in the UK so I'd a bird's-eye view of how Irish people had recorded life here, though his book is set before the boom at home: my experience was different, less traumatic, living in English cities felt less like a change and more like an extension and deepening of a familiar experience, a quickening experience of being away from something which still felt almost close enough to touch. I didn't want to fall into reminiscence, or to write about England as Other, as the old enemy, again notions familiar from the post-colonial Edward Said-style binary oppositions I'd studied in Galway.

But I was also interested in how British poetry, outside London and with exceptions like Douglas Dunn's *Terry Street* and Roy Fisher's Birmingham, seems very light on the poetry of place, of *social* or urban places, outside of London or the pastoral anyway. I wanted to lay out Manchester as usable material—I'm not planning on leaving—by writing poems like 'The Middle Kingdom', 'A Minute' and the set of 'destruction' poems which begins *Next Door*, 'A Pyramid Scheme', 'Diversion', and 'Moving In', poems which imagine a kind of reverse colonization. As *we* moved in, *they* moved to their holiday homes in the colonies. And I think, I hope, the book sounds equally strange, and maybe exotic, to Irish and non-Irish readers of the poems.

Can you say something about the impulse to catalogue, and the use of proper nouns? I am thinking especially about poems like 'The Middle Kingdom' and 'The Ice Carrier'. The poems seem to savour the strangeness of names. It seems to me, in these poems, to do with the newness of settling down and becoming a family: the poems are hoarding...

The great joy of having children is in the poems I hope. But there is also a completely new and vulnerable sense of mortality. Or so it appears to me, now: I wasn't conscious of that at the time but yes they are very caught up with gripping the here-and-now. Maybe that's also related to hoarding and the way they mark out and itemise the world around them.

Formally the catalogue or litany is something I love, though it's often associated with elegy and I'd become a little impatient with that elegiac note in my own poems, wanting instead a bit more tension and resistance: 'The Middle Kingdom' in particular puts some daylight between the more traditional subjects of a catalogue—flowers, birds, other artists, ships—and its looping list of different kinds of public and commercial premises in the industrial north. I meant it too as a kind of indirect companion to the Horace version.

Reading some of the poems of Next Door, I keep thinking of a line from Mahon's 'A Garage in County Cork': 'we might be anywhere but are in one place only...' I'm thinking especially of 'The Landing' and 'The Hundred Towns'. The end of the latter poem has changed since the book: a very Mahonesque thing to do! Can you explain your thinking behind the revision?

I wanted to set down what it felt like to live in a London which seemed comprised of millions of people like me, i.e., the English capital was inhabited by people from other places, the hundred towns of the title. Nancy's colleagues and our immediate neighbours in London were from all over, the US, Iraq, Iran, Pakistan, Botswana, Somalia, Sierra Leone—and I was teaching classes of teenagers who had blown in from the four corners of the world, all of them plugged into the same daily life but with disorienting hinterlands: one kid missed school because he and his father had been arrested breaking into the Iraqi embassy the day the Allied forces entered Baghdad. There's freedom, in the poem, in sitting in a park in sunny Greenwich, a feeling that you're disappearing right there at the centre of time, though all the while you're looking across the Thames at the Canary Wharf towers which the Provos bombed in 1996. Contemporary poetry, and Irish poetry, seemed to go out of focus in those cosmopolitan, global-feeling situations, but then you find there are resources for thinking about this, for asking: How much should you concede to the lure of the present moment? Or must a poem think of itself as historical, as an Irish *as opposed to* a London poem? It's a question that hung around in the background of 'The Hundred Towns' as I was revising or elaborating on it over 4 or 5 years, and—as Next Door neared completion—I must have felt the need to make that poem a little too thematic and bulldozing and schematic with the book version's mention of 'home', which the later version here avoids (I hope) while still bearing the theme in mind.

And, yes, that's a terrific and apt Mahon line, with a sense of potential *and* limit, a feeling that chimes with 'The Hundred Towns' and a lot else in Next Door. A couple of other points of contact with Mahon whose tone and phrasing are still a model to me: I must have had his London poems in view as well in 'The Hundred Towns'—I'm thinking of his Kensington poems, more than the brilliant and more recent Coleridge Biographia poem or the Jean Rhys poem which conjures up a more literary London; and Seamus Heaney thinks about the pull of metropolitan fashion in the 'District and Circle' sequence as well, though his London train is more decisively homeward bound and funereal.

You seem interested in interruption. The words of some celebrity in 'Interview' are cut off at a crucial moment; the asterisked numbers of a credit card form the title of a poem about tax and Wordsworth country; and the beautiful sonnet 'You Interrupt' gets interrupted and corrected mid-poem by a loved one.

I'd like to write poems which set different trains of thought in motion and entangle or untangle different images and ideas. And those gaps and interruptions and odd conjunctions are great prompters and inspirations to me and create that sense of change, of being caught off-guard. Not for a purposeful and obfuscatory ambiguity— and god knows there's plenty of that doing the rounds too—but in a way that keeps faith with the provisionality of writing, with the way poems dart and explore and discover as they explain what's what. 'Basically, there is no difference between understanding and pleasure', says music critic Charles Rosen—and I like poems which generate that act of understanding, which resist or draw the reader out initially, crossing from one narrowly conceived idiom into something broader and transforming. The idea of having a second speaker in a poem, the one who comes into 'You interrupt', becomes a very useful way of establishing tension and momentum, not so much as a sounding board but as a provocation or sceptical impetus to say more, to be clearer and more convincing, the poem as conversation, with the reader as a kind of omniscient eavesdropper.

When I teach workshops in Manchester I refer students to Proust's brilliant essay 'Against Sainte-Beuve' which discusses the way that certain moments and memories involuntarily catch you or interrupt your sense of 'how things are' and force you to sit down and re-examine who and where you are; and those blank spots or blind spots you mention reflect that. The credit card poem came out of re-reading Wordsworth after we moved to his world, the north of England: that poem, and 'Interview', both set up conventional lyric situations (I think) and try to escape from that tick-box form for something that's more mysterious, private and true, trying out some kind of combination of Wordsworth's spots of time with what CK Williams notices as 'the blank caverns of namelessness we encase'.

The poems here from Of All Places *have an even more acute sense of the foreignness of home. 'My Adolescence in New Zealand' remembers teenage out-of-place-ness and 'North Korea' seems to describe North Kerry! 'Aerialist' is that rarest of birds, a genuine Celtic Tiger poem, where Ireland is almost unrecognizable.*

Does any writer feel at home 'at home'? In Kerry, where those poems are set, there's an inbuilt foreignness, an inbetweenness to the place still, something I didn't understand until after I'd moved away: now, driving along the Cork-Kerry border in Sliabh Luachra, I know I'm almost home when I see the signpost for Ó Rathaille's 'stick' (i.e. hedge school). Ó Rathaille, and Eoghan Rua Ó Súilleabháin, are emblematic figures, eighteenth-century poets whose writing lives were split apart by the shift in power and language, but whose changing situations challenge the narratives of many accounts of Irish literature, whether it is Daniel Corkery's passionate synthesising account of a single national literature in Hidden Ireland or Thomas Kinsella's more pessimistic projection of Irish poetries in The Dual Tradition. Hartnett's

'Visit to Croom 1745' takes the Kinsella line, I think, when it travels the west Munster roads only to find the old estate a ruin and it was one model for 'North Korea', a poem which also draws on a friend's description of visiting Pyongyang; also from seeing, in the past few years, the weed-choked estates of new houses built during the boom at home, never lived in and unlikely to find tenants now the boom is over.

The poems also respond to the same idealised and more realist versions of the west that was part of the make-up of 'A Vision of Rahoon', trying to set down how things actually are and were even as they change around you, in the knowledge that there are wrongheaded and competing versions of this time and place abroad already. The estranging feeling and instability of, odd phrase, *returning home*, which is, I'd say, part of belonging anywhere, is magnified by bringing North Korea and New Zealand and the poor benighted Byelorussian circus into view in 'Aerialist'. The New Zealand poem is also a response to the New Zealand poet Bill Manhire who has published a typically oblique and sudden little poem called 'My Childhood in Ireland.'

The title poem, I recall you saying, is about the carpark in Villanova University in PA. Yes? Did the experience of being in the US, as Heimbold Chair of Irish Studies, have much of an impact on your work? More generally, how familiar or unfamiliar are the noises being made by American poets of our generation?

Yes, the six months in Villanova was a gift – the campus is in Bryn Mawr so we weren't too distracted by Philly's bright lights and we had terrible weather so I just hunkered down writing and revising the poems as a group. It's a longer book, with longer and more strongly narrative poems in it, because of the spell in Villanova.

There are two poems called 'Of All Places' in the book: one drills down into the history and prehistory of an unnamed place and the other pans across a lot of places which the poem joins together via those classic universal markers of modernity, the carparks. And the weather, so much snow, makes its way into the book too. I'd been reading Auden before I went, and spent a day or two in nearby Swarthmore reading through his restless drafts and lecture notes, reading his copy of his early poems which he rewrote for the first US edition of his poems: a note on one early poem said 'o god what rubbish'. And I visited Thomas and Eleanor Kinsella, who live part of the time in Philadelphia: amazing to walk into their mews house and find the le Brocquy *Tain* images on the wall, to see the poet at home in his work.

Reading, from outside, you develop a partial canon, a feel for certain useful or useable rhythms so I was looking at new books by August Kleinzahler, Robert Hass, Louise Gluck, Charles Wright, CK Williams, John Ashbery, Rodney Jones, poets I've read for a decade or more, and of course reading Muldoon in the US and talking to American poets about his work as a New Jersey-ite was interesting. I was lucky enough to get to know Daisy Fried and Sebastian Agudelo, two younger poets who have an unusual grip on actual day-to-day life and speech in their poems. They're not just stylists is what I mean and I'd like to think I'm interested in doing the same kinds of things in poems as they are. With a lot of the other American poets of my age I can't quite get a handle on the work on its own or maybe on my own terms: I can't tell whether they are virtuosic variations or just imitations of Ashbery or other American poets whose work I already like, but I do know I can't read them without reference to those older American poets. I did hear new sounds in Carl Phillips, in the beautiful and unexpected sentences and stanzas of *Speak Low*. And in Lisa Jarnot's *Night*

Scenes and Atsuro Riley's *Romey's Order* and I liked the gusto of Matthew Zapruder's *Come on all you ghosts.* I loved Jennifer Egan's *Goon Squad* novel and Aleksander Hemon's stories and *Lazarus Project* novel. Quick-witted, a little bit messy, direct, and written, or so it seemed, from the thick of their subjects, they make a good argument for writing.

A GOOD STORY

In the beginning was the conversation—the subject,
Your home: square fields, five-bar wooden gates,
An even sloping greenness, groves of larch and oak
Under which the animals rested or cropped at grass,
And all beneath a blue sky with a single tiny speck of cloud.

In the end, it was a meadow whitening in starlight
And a road reduced to stones of every size,
Potholes, dockleaves, encroaching bindweed,
Bees, ragwort, a rustling ditch by the side,
A line of grass through the middle

Tall and wild as your tales of the *Titanic*
And a sea-faring gran-aunt, the Chinese whispers
About the year 1900 and a one-way ticket
To Saigon, or was it Ceylon, a good story about
A bottle of smoke, the lost land, a litre of vodka

That required your health and a sigh, hushed,
Like the air in this overgrown passage that leads
Nowhere, for you are fragile as paper and your real estate
A stash of old currency and an expired blue passport
Inky and true with stamped dates and trade routes.

THE LONG WEEKEND

We set out before dark,
But late, and right on time
To join the after work

Traffic jams,
Nothing for it but to wait
Till they pull into dark homes

And clear the road at last.
We stop for nothing,
Drive at our pool of light,

Reach, by ten, the pier
And make our bright entrance
Into the canal's nightworld,

Which sleeves us in silence—
Midges on the water,
Fish biting ripples,

In the sedge a scatter
Of mallards and their drake.
A swan circles

And settles in our wake,
A pheasant whirrs overhead,
We chug from lock

To lock, between unlit fields
That look white and out of character:
Alone, for all the world,

We wave to each other
From the barge's
Prow and tiller,

Nothing between us,
Such sweet exchange,
And time ticking over, urgent

As the rented, well-oiled engine.

A VISION OF RAHOON

What's left:
Schtumpig terriers, unchained big dogs
And stray cats that yowl at night,
First light, noon, dusk.

Outside of the stoat
Dead beside the boilerhouse,
Bloated with the blue poison
I set last week,
No animals enter the wrecked yard

Though worms
Crawl from the moist shadow

Under the cement tyre
When the wind keels over the clothes tree.

The birds are my noisy company:
Tits, magpies, the occasional crow,
And then the furious jingle jangle
Of the finch and the so-called songbirds,
The blackbird and the thrush.

Since I've started keeping to my room,
Truth be told, there is not much life
In this burnt-out estate, the towers
Sagged by dynamite to their knees,
Their people dispersed
In the wasteland of outlying developments.

At night, when a bird
Would tuck his head under his wing,
I take out the wine
(Rhubarb, potato, elderberry)
And drink toast after toast to the dead,
The not-forgotten, absent friends,
The rain frying on the slate roof.

NIGHTJAR

Everyone knew about it before long,
My mother's mother's return
To Newmarket from Hong Kong
With her policeman, his pension

And, stranded with them, her ayah,
Who with her eyes closed and no one about
Would burn orange peel on the Aga
And kept one other personal habit,

Hanging washed jars off the ash trees
In her family's back garden
Where they'd outstare the neighbours
Like some never-seen-before bird.

GOING PLACES

It doesn't happen often. Stuck in my room, say,
Looking at rain or for a book, seeing that the floor may
Need hoovering, hungover possibly,
Re-arranging the postcards on the wall:
                                    At times like this
I begin to remember childhood afternoons,
Sitting in the backseats of cars, going places,
Telephone wires on either side, like fences
For giant invisible horses.

MEDIUM WAVE

To enter the kingdom, be prepared . . .

On the midnight run from the capital
The woman across the aisle
Takes out one earphone and shouts hoarsely
'We've come into Radio Kerry'

At the fluoresced half-empty carriage,
Our reflections asleep together in the black glass
Through hours of static which re-emerge
As local notes, the results and the deaths.

AFRICA

Heat rises, palpably, having scorched and cracked the earth.
In the distance, unreal as a cloud, a mountain looms;
A few kids amble by with shorts on and nothing else.
At night, at their watering holes, I listen to their fathers:
'If this weather doesn't break . . .', 'It's like bloody Africa.'

TODAY'S IMPERATIVE

after Horace, Ode 1:7

Others have herblife, bogland, the bird sanctuary.
Or manmade canals and urban decay.

And they have international flights of fancy too:
But wherever they go,

It all looks and sounds the same to me,
Mountains, some work, a nice sunrise that none of the other tourists sees

Or an epiphany that signals a deeper
Engagement with the local patois/native literature.

Then there are the argonauts
Who labour in the interstices of a language, or two at most;

And that crowd whose ambition is to introduce gender
To the reader who hasn't got one on her:

Long warm-ups, agreed movements from *a* to *b*, and put up the
shutters
With a lyrical turn or various little-known fabrics and figures,

Such as you often find in those who use family detail as glitter
To stud the rough black rock of their fictions.

And I like all this, but
It doesn't live in me, it doesn't wake me up in my skin at night.

I'd rather sing to you about what's imperative,
So, listen. Take your mind off the stresses and anxiety of life

And whether you're in a southern town
Like Cork or Montpellier, or even Washington or Rome—

Go pour yourself a glass of wine.
Now. Imagine the kind of man who trusts himself to fortune

And says: 'Let us go wherever it takes us.
We've heard that a better life awaits us *and* we've seen worse.

Today, banish worry, exile it, the night's young now
And soon we'll be back to the grind, in fact, maybe tomorrow . . .'

ACTION

It is 3 a.m., on a wet night, and I'm stood
In the middle of a field,
Listening to *The Open Mind*, a repeat, on a walkman
When Corman with his wand and loudspeaker cone
Directs me, 'Hey you', and then the long arm,
To walk across the field,
And to wade into the river
With the boom close to the water.
This is experience and I need experience.

EFFECTS

On my one visit to your bijou apartment—
Glass, wood, neutral tones—you went on
And on about important places you'd lived in,
Then hushed the room to listen
To a bitter night in wartime Berlin

When snow unmapped streets
Outside a hall bright with human heat
Where an orchestra played Mozart
And a choir sight-read sheets
That gave the text a fresh start,

'Hic in terra' for 'in Jerusalem',
'Deus in coelis' for 'Deus in Sion'.
Through the static, the boys' voices sound divine
And the crowd listen as if *Requiem*
Was made with their night in mind.

You refilled our glasses and whispered
In my ear. As the announcer declared
'That was . . .' you flicked on your CD,
'Epic Effects', first up a yowling Arctic wind
Rushed up my spine, then cold

Wincing rain, a thunderstorm that
Set me a-bristle like a cat
And your *pièce de résistance*, an at-
Om bomb that I hear yet,
All jangle and unnatural collapse

With stringed seconds of nothing,
Then the whole bone china tea-cup asunder,
A swinging door creaking open.
What night could go further?
I said my piece, not that you'd hear anything,

And I walked home, in the rain and wind,
Wondering at what exact point
The day becomes night
In a landscape like that, like this, light
Disappearing from what's still left behind.

A PYRAMID SCHEME

An old Cortina's come to rest
at the end of the road. The weeks pelt
its glass and steel, invisibly
emptying it and making free

with some random person
who strips the interior and then,
accompanied, helps himself
to tyres, battery, driveshaft, exhaust.

The bodywork flakes and scabs.
Going nowhere, looking naked, mad,
mirrorless and windowless,
it gathers accessories

like one of those disused roadside crannies:
plastic bags, a seatful of empties
and, adjacent, a holed mattress, a pallet,
a small fridge—the whole lot useless, inside out,

till the rusting shell starts half-stories,
the kind that make it first notorious,
for the children who will have to learn
what goes on at night, or could go on,

then a shelter for their elders,
a try-out zone, its vacant doorless
frame a guarded hiding place, its fag-end
still paying a dividend.

MOVING IN

Her garden, once a selling point, is a state already.
Its furthest, dampest end is conifers, debris
and constant dark. And it's a zoo of noise,

sucking road and sky into the old semi's acoustic shadow.
There used to be one long bed of cultivated earth,
planted with care and effort,
where she—the last owner-occupier—
matched each half-season to a different colour

so that one unknown variety ceded ground
to another unheralded
profusion of whites or reds or blues,
much as her post continues
to arrive, credit card and book club promotions
giving way to seasonal round robins
bearing good news, best wishes and written postscripts
from the colonies' retiring outposts.

Now I hardly step or look outdoors,
riveted by the school and fiscal years'
eternal returns, but unable to ignore
how one good neighbour or another
declares with careless, proprietary accent,
'She loved that garden', as I half-plan
uprooting even the roses to put in
here a slide, and there a swing.

DIVERSION

I noticed it day one and then forgot
the redbrick viaduct

till the Council boys
in the luminous hardhats and vests

raised scaffolding that cast shadows
straight and precise

as a map of the colonies
across the footpath and the green margin

where they've stacked the new sleepers
and earthed the transformer.

THE STREET

Lee's car has sat on blocks at least six weeks.
He rolls off the tarp and we stand around his yard.
His friend Amit, he reckons it's the sparks.
Then Mr Kumar shuffles by, leaning on his stick,
with a can of petrol. He feeds it into his *Bluebird*,
straightens up and says, 'Nice day. Will get hotter.'
The rubbish is beginning to stink. The Council's on strike.
Kids suddenly mill around, chasing after
one another, and then they're gone again.
We mind our own business, no one says anything.
Mr Kumar enters his front garden,
gone a bit to seed, and the lawn needs mowing.
We pretend we are all looking at Lee's defunct car,
me, Lee, Amit, even David whose window clicks
open across the street. It's melting; is it the sun
that's stopped moving, or us? Mr Kumar darkens the front door,
faces up to its fish-eye lens, fingers his useless key
and presses the bell. The street goes quiet and sounds empty.
It seems to wait a minute, as if something

is about to repeat itself, even though there's no sign yet
of that door snapping open, of Mrs Kumar
with a stick or a rolled-up paper to fold and switch the air
around her husband's bowed and balding head, no sign
of his noise that goes nowhere but will fetch the large white van
and a policewoman, no sign either of how we'll start again
to speak to Mr Kumar about the weather, or the state of the road
and the chances of driving it in his *Bluebird* or Lee's *Colt*.

THE MIDDLE KINGDOM: A DIRECTORY

For Receptions, Occasions and Venues, see the University, the Contact, Urmston Masonic Hall. 'Bowl a maiden over at the Lancashire County Cricket Club.' See Wedding Services. See Food. See Photos and Videos. See Clothes and Appearance. See Transport. See Religious Organizations.

For Religious Organizations, see also Churches, Church Halls and Places of Worship. See Church Furnishings and Supplies.

For Church Furnishings, see Reclaimers and Architectural Antiques. See also, Builders' Merchants, Demolition, Roofing Materials, Salvage and Reclamation, Masons.

For Masons, see Monumental Masons, Memorial Stone Masons, Drystone Wallers and Sculptors.

For Sculptors, see Pop Empires and Bright Morning Star (Or widen search). For Bright Morning Star, see also under Calligraphy.

For Calligraphy, see Books, Rare and Secondhand, Factory Shops and Villages (See also Further Education; See Universities). See also Shopping Centres. See Decorations.

For Decorations, see Costumes, see Fancy Dress, Theatrical Supplies, Uniforms and Staff Wear.

For Uniforms and Staff Wear, see also Marking and Other Identity
Services, see Barcodes, see Rubber Stamps, see Security Services and
Equipment.

For Security Services and Equipment, see also Intercom Systems.
See Closed Circuit TV and VTR. See Hi-fi. See Gifts.

For Gifts, see Flowers, see Garden Centres (See Nurseries, see Dec-
orations), see also China and Glass (Crystal). See Wedding Services. See
also Places of Worship, Church Furnishings, Masons, Sculptors, Dec-
orations, Flowers. See The Moon Under Water for England's Finest
Venues and Occasions. See The Chorlton Conservative Club, see The
Black Lion (No Reception).

INTERFERENCE

I step into it as it surrounds me,
a patch of earth so hemmed in by trees
the branches meet over my head.
Another person, like a curtain in a sick ward,
draws the little light into her interfering voice.
What she says is nothing new:
'It will all come out in the wash.'
A stout short woman, of high colour,
she must drink alone at night
with that same narrow look of desire.

Will she still be there—a secret keeper—afterwards?
She'd said, 'I'm keeping my eye on you.'
I thought I saw her at an uncle's funeral,
and that day we moved house. I like to hear

little or nothing about her.
All this time, too, I feel
the damp heat rising out of the earth,
the wind shaking down the trees.

TINNITUS

My father's tinnitus is like the hiss off a water cooler,
only louder. And it doesn't just stop like, say, a hand-dryer—the worst is
it comes and goes. Or you shine a light on it
and it looks permanent as the sea,

a tideless sea that won't go away. The masker
he's been prescribed is a tiny machine, an arc of white noise
that blacks out a lot
but can't absorb the interference totally

any more than you or I—taking the air,
stirring milk into coffee, daydreaming through the six o'clock news,
trying to sleep on a wet night—
can simply switch off what's always there, a particular memory

nagging away, the erosive splash off a little river
wearing away the road, say, on the Connor Pass,
a day out, through which he'd accelerate
in the flash, orange Capri.

BY ACCIDENT

The night our boy fell I was running late.
I made the unanswered call
under the city's bright,
then cloudy, skull
and, as the needle knows the north,

trembled at the shock ahead,
a house blacked-out and silent,
a night that, commuted,
ran to earth in accident,
a shorted circuit, you and he locked

into the diagnostic dark
in Park Royal intensive care
where consequences arc
beyond 'contusion', 'fracture',
the ward's humming network

to a different city, a year later,
the kind of night, calm, almost tranquil,
when he calls and haggles with his sister
even as we find more and more unreal
our imaginings, which were terrible.

YOU INTERRUPT

Purr and whistle, a change of gears,
the milk float, next-door's shift *and* the chorus
of robin, tit and blackbird: all have read
our waking up. 'Nearly 5,' you said,
'and it's already bright.' The children stirred,
but didn't wake: things could be worse.
Real coffee for an early start. The word
for this is long-lost, beyond use: it'll be years,
and what harm, before it gets a chance.
You interrupt, 'It's not like this:
it's the same as before'; birdsong, the steaming kettle . . .
Upstairs first one, then the other begins to call.
Is this enough? Will that be alright?
You'll go in a while; the traffic's still light.

✳✳✳✳ ✳✳✳✳ ✳✳✳✳ 5443

I'm held in the second bar
of the Revenue's *Casio* solo,
the hot receiver at my ear,
drumming the stairs with my free hand,
on my lap a sheaf of credit card statements,
like a book of lyrics,
each with a number and date, some named:
The Lime Tree, The Bookshop, Dove Cottage.
Dove Cottage: it's like I'm miles away,

not many moons ago, escaping a traffic jam,
walking up that dusty, cobbled sidestreet,
a dwarf orchard at one corner,
music too, from an open doorway,
money in my pocket, time on my hands.

THE LANDING

I live for the wrong turns—
    a conversation about Canada
or Labour veering into
    how no one'd rather
be invisible than fly;
    the names of the trees
that shadow the walk home
    go missing among
Hollywoods and statins, then
    who'll pick up the children,
and where will we live?

    The past's a decrepit hotel: knock it,
we should inherit nothing . . .
    Maybe, you say, Hereford
and environs
    resemble nowhere more
than Waterford,
    the sort of dark place
where nothing has ever,

ever happened:
   I know this place well,
      working slowly backwards

to what I expect
   and least anticipate.

THE HUNDRED TOWNS

There is no capital of the world
CZESLAW MILOSZ,
'Bypassing Rue Descartes'

We negotiate
   ring road, tunnel and ferry
      but by noon GMT

are nowhere, ie, an endless suburb
   stacked and balanced
      like washing up.

Our day out seems set to fray
   into a relief map of noise
      the kids crying *where*

until I call a halt
   and we abandon the car
      and follow a sign pointing north:

we reach the beaten path, tar and mud,
    and trundle buggies up blind, rising corners,
        piggyback past tourists consulting an A-Z

and a man with children who smiles
    at the sight of us:
        'another day in paradise . . .'

In a mile, an hour, we lay out the picnic,
    a tartan rug on the side of a hill,
        greenly adrift in the public park:

a barbeque smokes the wind,
    a lean-to of a caff
        hosts wake-up karaoke, blues and big band

(someone murders "It's oh so quiet"),
    quad bikes buzz and weave
        earning a crowd with their figures of eight

and across the river Canary Wharf glitters,
    a sky-high shower curtain
        in the rainless weather.

Quick clouds flit in the sky's corners.
    flat out in the heat like a film,
        the city's empty, the future of a hundred towns.

The kids run off; we share a cold and fizzy beer,
    but I close my eyes as you say, 'we could not,
        would not be anywhere but here'

and I sleep off this well-planned afternoon
    from which, not soon enough, we'll double back
        anonymous as anyone

mistaking signposts in the glowing night.

THE END OF THE WORLD

A desk, three chairs, some paper,
paper clips, two elastic bands, a hole puncher.
A mini stapler. A note to say
a computer is on its way.
A fold-up map of the city centre,
an instruction manual for a printer. No printer.
A phone, a bin. And in the bin there's
a black plastic strip that bears
the name and title of the previous occupant.
A feeling that nothing will happen
if I don't pick up when my number is called,
if I idle at the desk instead
looking at the tangle of strings
that might operate the blinds,
thinking about a pun, or a metaphor,
and how,
            as a matter of fact,
it's not the end of the world.

A MIDGIE

I pick a midgie out of my red wine.
The garden goes greener in the lilac time.
This will go down on the permanent record.
A night is nothing if not its own reward.
The foxgloves corked with bees.
The snail outlining a life of ease.
The black things wait. Or may never show.
That's innocent. I know, I know.

MY ADOLESCENCE IN NEW ZEALAND

for Bill Manhire

I didn't want to go to bed and then
I didn't want to get up. The men,
my uncles and father, planned to watch
the international, a grudge match,
on the new remote-controlled TV.
I was beginning to get ideas about coffee.
I sniffled and coughed, my nose in a book.
The *Rainbow Warrior* turned into Helen Clark.
Those days we worried about serious things.
I was never into *The Lord of the Rings*.
I preferred biographies of polar explorers:
a long journey and evidence of errors
disappearing like a snowflake in Antarctica,
a dropped knife tuning up for the orchestra.

AERIALIST

i.m. Vitaly Kharapavitski

I'd talked us all back to Ireland, a week in Killorglin and a plan
to take shovel, bucket, armbands and an inflatable fin,
a picnic basket and a tartan rug to a different beach
each mid-morning. It was quiet and all worked out, so much
we might have dreamed it and never gone—except
that one day we parked on Inch Strand and ploughed it up
as the tide around us did what it does.

Cooped up inside at night was a different prospect
in a rental no one could pretend was Bali or Venice.
For entertainment, ice-cream vans and posters for a circus,
not exactly an infrastructure. The 'Royal Russian Circus':
20 euro a head. I cursed the Celtic Tiger and paid, cash at the till,
wishing briefly I'd stayed, done an MBA and, some violence
to the language, lived it deal by deal.

Every artist looks after his own props. The balloon
'exploded into flames', the cage fell, then the heavy steel ball.
Becoming witnesses, one or two hundred people
thought it was part of the act, fire as magic, whoosh and clatter,
nothing irregular in the mid-air routine.
The reports say he was Belorussian, 26, a clown or
'an aerialist in a clown costume'. And that he threw his wife clear.

We'd seen, in Rosbeigh, pre-show and a week earlier,
hanging around, nerveless and going nowhere an elephant,

a giraffe and, between them, a zebra. Canvas and steel
were shaped into a marquee. And from behind Coomasaharn
glider after glider hung in the sky, coasting away clear to the north.
A new bungalow advertised art, another a scuba school
and night-kayaking in the phosphorescent ocean

by which that night, stars and stripes on each enormous brow,
the elephants balanced on buckets like shuttlecocks,
while the giraffe nodded, stately and gawky, and a shabby lion
  made his unheard-of roar, still a memory on each nearby farm.
  A crowd of method actors, the circus animals, though
  instead of a tiger the MC, for the sake of form,
  squirted water at us from a flower between acts.

The 'Sadovs' had performed for one year and had one stunt:
in it he couldn't find her, she fooled and hid,
the story so simple we gripped the wooden ringside,
grinding our heels into the matted grass and, would it ever end,
opened our mouths like parents as he kept
falling over and out of the hot-air balloon. Over
and over he went, *poor man*, who would throw his wife clear.

Weeks later, and back across the water, I saw online
the Dublin owner of the Royal Russians, or its spokesman,
speak of close-knit community, the harness, the hoist,
and the families of the deceased and bereaved flying over.
It seemed for a while, here, as if things might be as they were,
autumn closing in, a net that at the last moment would come apart
taking only the leaves from the trees and the name of the year.

NORTH KOREA

Time is not wasted in your subtle temples.
Warm air from the south blows about
your rusting trees, a fine dust settles
on the new shop's lintel and on the local
of the regular and the fly by night.

The weather thins out, turns unseasonal
and makes a word of the ditches' rustling,
an expression that escapes us, a smattering
of another language. The road crumbles
at each new estate's stone-clad entrance.

No one drives anything out of there.
It plays the part of its life, just once,
to retired horses and standing stones.
At the junction no one will hear
a whisper about the coming year.

OF ALL PLACES

Even in Kyoto / hearing the cuckoo's cry / I long for Kyoto. BASHO

It takes imagination, crossing the car park, to long for
the car park, to miss in its empty numbered spaces
the pluming suspensions of another day, to see
cracks in this sidewalk wrinkle into a cold, western night

bearing coke, Silk Cut and Hula Hoops to a waiting room,
checking on you as you check a bleep, talking through
the drunks, the snifflers and the relatives,
talking into existence the work-life balance,
our imagined oceanic air, streets we'd walk
and occasionally lift our heads to look around at,
the teeming air above our social heads,
a future as much a fact as the hills and villages
we left and never knew—you and I, now and then
(car parked in the unforgotten outskirts),
walking through the city dark, away and toward,
dreaming of moving, next to one another.

Maurice Riordan

What is the earliest poem in this selection? Can you remember when and where it was written, and in what spirit? More particularly, what do you recall of Ireland and its poetry at the moment of composition, and of how you defined your creative ambitions starting out?

'Rural Electrification'. It dates from 1984 or 85 when I'd come over to London—high-tailed it out of Cork with my girlfriend on a Slattery bus. Ireland was a nasty place those years—as was Maggie's Britain, but that didn't upset me so much. I think the best poems about Ireland in the 80s were then being written by Paul Durcan, things like 'The Haulier's Wife', semi-surreal narratives of strange invention and humour. But *that* Paul was no danger to me, no influence. Paul Muldoon was. His effect on young male British and northern Irish poets was overwhelming at the time. And I was trying to stay on my feet. In Irish terms, I was self-consciously a Mahon-man, and I was also trying to catch things from English poets (Larkin) and American poets (Bishop, Dobyns), and from fiction writers (Flannery O'Connor, Carver, Munro, McEwan, Peter Carey's *The Fat Man in History*), just about anything that gave me some protection from the strong winds blowing from the general direction of Lough Neagh. But I wasn't doing so good. I'd very nearly given up, in fact, when I began attending a small workshop in Notting Hill, run by Robert Greacen. I was restarting but slowly. This was one of the poems I showed there.

Did you start writing at UCC? It must have been a pretty lively time when you were there, with Greg Delanty and Patrick Crotty and Tom McCarthy around then? Were you also contemporaries with the Innti group?

My first flush of writing had happened when I was an undergraduate at UCC. I haven't collected those poems but their effect has stayed with me. They were too precipitate for someone with no technique. It's best to start on the practice ground.

As a teaching institution, UCC was poor in those days—a memorably forgettable experience for eager English students. If I had my time back, I would have done Irish—and so indeed might have become involved with Innti poets like Michael Davitt and Nuala Ní Dhomnaill, with whom I had only slight contact. Or if I really had a second chance, I'd have gone to Trinity or further afield. But there were compensations. John Montague arrived during my second year, and he facilitated some famous readings. I remember chauffeuring the elderly Hugh MacDiarmid, and his wife Valda, around in my mother's yellow Mini in a doomed search for Midleton, the whiskey, that is—which he said was his favourite. Robert Graves came to read, as well as such lesser lights as Seamus Heaney, Michael Longley, and the 21-year-old Paul Muldoon. There was a lively undergraduate poetry scene. Paul Durcan was studying Archaeology. He is a wonderful reader of his poems, but I remember him then whispering them with inaudible intensity. There was Sean Dunne and Gregory O'Donoghue, both of whom died young—I became close to Gregory when in Canada. And there was Tom McCarthy, Theo O'Dorgan, Patrick Crotty. Greg Delanty came along later.

Much of the landscape of your childhood must have been very similar to Heaney's and Muldoon's? That must have been very difficult starting off, to find some free space there. One image in 'Rural Electrification' seems to play knowingly with at least two competing allusions: Heaney's 'Digging' with its 'milk in a bottle / corked sloppily with paper,' and Muldoon's line from 'Quoof': 'red hot half-brick in an old sock...'

It's a Wellington sock, isn't it? Which is a thick wool sock, so it's handy for keeping the tea warm. The detail would have been important to me, just as a way of claiming the validity of my own experiences. The way of life I knew as a child was similar to what Heaney and Muldoon knew and had already written poems about. At the primary level of the senses, we'd seen and heard many of the same things. We'd used the same soap, said the same prayers, went to the same schools, had the same 'mother'. It was a homogenous culture—that rural Catholic nationalist world. But for Heaney and Muldoon there was the electric tension of division, of sectarianism, and being under the whip. Down my way, in the immediate vicinity round where I grew up, a Protestant was as rare, and notable, as a Bugatti.

I realized part of the job for me was to find my own space. It wasn't easy. But then I think difficulty is no bad thing. I might have written more freely, and more poems, if Seamus Heaney had never been born—or if he'd gone on the African missions. But I suspect the poems I have written, or some of them, are more interesting because of a degree of resourcefulness and reinvention they required. Even so, not least in the 1980s, the last thing anyone in England wanted was another male Irish poet writing about his childhood. There used to be a sign up in Queen Square 'No Irish Poets Wanted'. Only joking.

In A Word from the Loki Ireland is already at arm's length. I'm thinking especially of 'Indian Summer', which remembers visiting London, and 'Long Distance', set in North America. Was leaving always a foregone conclusion?

There was a generational shift around 1970 in Ireland, as the 60s arrived along with an economic spring tide. Youngsters like myself starting university had summer jobs and the new higher education grant, thank you. People were off all over the place, long-haired, marching, guitar-strumming, the lucky ones sharing sleeping-bags. I made the famous trip to London in September 1972, and spent five years in Canada—a barren time for my poems—from 1976–81. So yes, a few years later, I drew on those experiences for my first viable poems. 'Long Distance' is about those days living in Hamilton, Ontario, close to the US border. But it was a few years on again, when life in London had acquired some layers for me as well as domestic complication, that my writing began to prosper. By then I was in my mid-thirties. I really was a slow-starter.

'Time Out' and 'Last Call' are the poems in the first book most obviously drawing on models other than the obvious Irish ones. The long lines, the play on urban myth . . . Is there an American influence in these poems, like CK Williams?

CK Williams, yes, I read *Flesh and Blood* in 1988 or '89, and later the poems in *Tar*, which I admire rather more. Also, Stephen Dobyns, from whose 'Tomatoes'—a terrific poem—I took the epigraph for 'Time Out'. It was a happening time for my poetry. I was on a little roll with domestic poems, like 'Milk', that began with 'Last Call' in 1989 and ended for me in June 1992 with 'Time Out'. I'd realized that poems were fictions—and I saw the poems I was writing were fictional tangents to my own experience. Finding one of those tangents got me started. I think one took it for granted poems should have the prose virtues, be clear and fresh and spoken, though the American influences underlined that. The other thing for me was the formal integrity of the poem, that it have the same genetic identity in every syllable. It should be like a stick of Brighton rock someone has said, but I forget who. And sensing that form, and then bringing it about, was what excited and satisfied me about writing poems.

I was attending a workshop those years—well, the same one as before but now Matthew Sweeney was the gaffer. We met in his flat in Dombey Street and later on upstairs in the Lamb pub around the corner. As happens this workshop has become somewhat mythologized. We didn't meet that often, 3 or 4 times a year, and even then not everyone was a regular. But the 'Lamb group' included Jo Shapcott, Mike Donaghy, Lavinia Greenlaw, Eva Salzman, Charles Boyle, among others . . . Cahal Dallat, Tim Dooley, Vicki Feaver. Don Paterson came a few times. It was very important for me. Some of the poets were established, others were rising stars. It was a testing-ground for my work just at the right time.

The title poem and 'Some Sporting Motifs' have a very similar voice that seems unlike anything in Irish poetry, like a documentary voiceover. It reminded me of Flann O'Brien. Where were you going with that voice, and where does it come from?

Good question—which is to say I don't know the answer. My best guess is that it's a version of a distancing dispassionate voice, or tone, you find elsewhere in the poems. That objective voice is up-front in the poems you mentioned; in other poems perhaps it is more disguised, or they seem confessional.

Perhaps an indication of this is that 'Time Out' and 'A Word from the Loki' were actually written back to back. Well, the Loki poem was written steadily over ten days, and when it was finished, then I wrote the other straight off. Clearly, the two are connected in my brain some place, but I don't know where—and no reason I should know, I guess. A similar thing happened with *Floods*, where I wrote the title-poem steadily over several weeks, and then one morning sat down and wrote 'The Sloe' onto the screen quickly and without it seeming to ask for revisions.

Is composing into a computer a usual composition process? Is there a relationship between that and the fact that a number of the poems from Floods *take the form of a single sentence? 'The Sloe' in particular is a magnificent high-wire act over three and a half pages.*

I use paper and screen about equally nowadays. Everyone has their own habits and spooks. Mine is I'm put off by fresh clean paper, especially those nice notebooks people give you for Christmas and so on. I used to write always in cheap school exercise books—many drafts, and writing it out fully each time. I've written sometimes on big envelopes or the back of typed drafts. That's where I wrote 'Time Out'. Now I often start with a notebook, move to the screen, and sometimes back to paper again, if there is a problem. Writing remains a messy physical activity for me. But the screen is a great reusable canvas. And I think it does encourage me to spread myself a bit—and also actually not to rely on certain forms. Sonnets and villanelles are ideal 'page' poems. I doubt I could have written 'The Sloe' on paper—unless I was using a toilet roll!

Most specifically, there seems to be a relationship between the single-sentence poems like 'The Sloe' and 'Silk' and time. In another interview, you gave the one-word answer 'Time' in response to the question: 'What are your poems about?' Can you say something about time in these poems, and also in 'The Dinner Call'?

Time, yes. I think I partly meant narrative, or fictional, time—the ways one can play around with it in poems [as well as other fictions]. Once you're into the age of film, then you have useful models or metaphors for replaying, stopping, reversing time, and so forth. I confess I take childish pleasure in seeing the hat pop back onto the head, that sort of thing. MacNeice used these filmic things brilliantly in a few poems, and they have been very influential, especially 'Soap Suds' . . . I think a few poets keep that one running in the background, as I do.

It also interests me that no-one knows what time is—or if it IS anything. And our brains are not good with processing our experience of it. You reach a time in life when things that happened long ago seem near, and recent things are distant. In 'The Sloe', and the other two poems, I guess you have some of that. The eponymous sloe became edible the night the ice-man died, 5000 years ago. But it's still edible. No change, so no time has passed—not for the sloe, not for the ice-man.

Time is an entirely relative concept. 5,000 years encompasses all of historical memory but would just about figure in the life of a glacier. It doesn't count at all in geological time. Equally, very tiny durations can be momentous—the decision, the insight, the irreversible action. These are for us humans perhaps what 'real' time is, what the Greeks called *kairos* as opposed to *chronos*, the ordinary stuff. I guess you could say poems occupy, or partake of, *kairos*, and that is what you have in 'The Dinner Call', where the proto-poem, the actual dinner-call, is freed from chronological time.

I find time is a component of a poem, like rhythm or tone or register—that's to say the handling of it is part of the overall effect. And a sentence is an important way of handling it, since it suspends time. Okay, time passes while you read, but if the sentence is good enough, our brain cannot check until it is released by the completion of the sentence. And within that duration you can manipulate time, stretch it, compress it, overlay one type of time on another, and so on. It doesn't have to be a sentence, of course—it's more likely to be Henry James or a French film. But poems like to do things in purest form.

Time is central to 'On Not Experiencing the Ultraviolet Catastrophe' and 'The Wineglass', both of which use a romantic setting to meditate on quantum mechanics.

Not that I know much about quantum mechanics! Though I did for years find that stuff fascinating. I think I swing back and forth between a quasi-spiritual experience of the world and a purely physical one. That latter, the sense of vast and also minute energies, including those of our bodies, and brains, sometimes feels vivid and as if hyper-real. It's exhilarating and also frightening. The idea of love like that, as a vivifying but dangerous force, was expressed by the Latin poet Lucretius. It is an unconsoling view—but also, as an experience, irresistible. It is literally so, since it takes over the system . . . chemically, I suppose, and can poison and kill you. So, those poems in *Floods* are my shot at registering that. The ultraviolet one, for instance, makes play with 'radiance' and why it's not actually annihilating. 'Southpaw' confuses gender and appears to find physical indeterminacy erotic. Another of those metaphysical poems, 'Caisson', re-imagines love in a world where light doesn't figure, or is not the primary source of sensation, and so we visualize experience through sound waves. They are poems that approach love with a speculative curiosity. Is it not an odd disruptive thing, they say, and they look at it in the arena of the strange and powerful forces of the universe, as we know them, or as we're supposed to know them from quantum physics and current cosmological thinking. There's hopefully some irony, of course, a kind of pervasive skepticism coming across. What *do* we know about time, matter, psychology? As creatures we seem to be exquisitely equipped to pick up signals, to sense stuff. We're great feelers! But have no idea what's going on. We're pretty good at jumping to conclusions but remain quite blind to outcomes. One phase of life seems to show you one thing, you think you're sorted, then the next phase displaces it, and on we go.

Floods *also has a gorgeous translation from the Irish of Sean Ó'Ríordáin, 'Frost'.* *Munster poets always seem much closer to Irish, more likely to find their influences in Irish. Sean Ó'Ríordáin seems to have been very important.*

The perception may be unfair to poets such as Austin Clarke and Thomas MacDonagh, who historically tried to forge a bridge with the Gaelic past, and of course Synge and Flann O'Brien, too, if you count them. Among the living, Muldoon has done many wonderful translations. I think Ciaran Carson grew up speaking Irish. What is true is that there are areas of the south and west where the Irish tradition is still in the air. Its lore and its music are all around and English— or Hiberno-English—feels like a flimsy disguise. Michael Harnett switched from English to Irish in the 70s. It was a drastic thing for a poet to do, but in orienting himself to his native place, West Limerick, it was not illogical.

As for myself, growing up in East Cork, what I sensed was the *absence* of words for many of the familiar birds and plants. Okay, everyone knew crows and robins, but not say a stonechat or a goldcrest. They were just 'birds'. As for plants, an awful lot was covered by the word 'weeds'. Sometimes people used the Irish words, or a corruption of them, but really the disappearance of Irish just two or three generations before had left a hole in people's knowledge of the world around them. Larkspur, coltsfoot, spurrey, meadowsweet, woodruff, brooklime . . . I was introduced to those words by the labels on drums of ICI weedkiller, or spray cans as we called them. I think that may have set me off on a different trail. I sometimes regret not knowing Irish better and not having the chance to speak it during my long sojourn with the Saxon. But that's 'the bundle of accident and incoherence' who sits down for his cornflakes. As a poet, you could say I've stuck with the spray cans, and remained in thrall to the variousness and suppleness of a language which is also, of course, my mother tongue.

Ó'Ríordáin was a presence when I was at UCC. We knew some of his poems from school, so this was the first time I beheld a poet in the flesh. He was—still is arguably—the biggest fish in a Munster jersey. He is a poet with an intense, perhaps narrow, modern mind whose idiom is both contemporary and traditional. Not a million miles from Larkin in that way, in fact, but also a link to an immemorial past—well much more than a link, an actual outpost of it and a sort of reproach to oneself. He's a tough nut for the would-be translator. I was glad with 'Frost' to have perhaps cracked it, if only the once.

There seems to be an Irish model also in the 'Idylls' sequence that is at the heart of your third collection, The Holy Land. *I've heard you talk about how the second section of that sequence was originally prompted by the 'music of what happens' story from the Fenian Cycle. Can I ask you to say something about the attraction of the prose sequence and that note of elegy in 'Frost' carried forward with into the third book?*

I started on the idylls in a very specific way. There is a prose poem in John Montague's 1974 *Faber Book of Irish Verse* called 'The Finest Music' involving Fionn Mac Cumhaill and his band. It's actually an extract from James Stephens' *Irish Fairy Tales*, and it's there because Sean Lucy, who was then Professor of English at UCC, was fond of it and brought it to JM's attention. I did an imitation of it, just doodling really—but then rather liked what occurred. So I carried on and did several more in a similar vein. Before long I had the bulk of that prose sequence. I was a bit nonplussed, to be honest, as I'm not in fact a big fan of prose poems, not in English anyway, as they often seem a bit precious. But I did feel these were different, partly because of the narrative emphasis, and also because of their use of dialogue. The dialogue is oblique, coded at times and almost cryptic. That's exactly the kind of conversation I grew up with—it is in my mother tongue—and I got a kick out of doing it.

The elegiac aspect is specific, too. The family farm is 12 miles outside Cork city, that is to say it was a world away up until the late 60s, and even then a place you might easily miss in your travels. But that changed around the turn of the millennium. My mother died then, so the farm no longer *belonged* to me and my children. Also that part of the county got drawn into the network of the city, with zoning, new roads, and so on, and indeed a few of the now notorious housing estates got built in the area. I wanted to recreate it as a place of work and conviviality, of lore, animals, crops—a place too with its own brand of humour and a habit of speech that is distinct in its pace and music and turn of phrase. I did it with a strong feeling that such things could never again be part of the life of the place.

You can't write that kind of nostalgia, though, without some sort of lens, or arrangement of lenses. I was aware of that. Fionn and his loquacious followers wandering around ancient Ireland were one kind of refraction—as were the Apostles in Galilee. But I tried to keep in play the whole tradition of pastoral elegy back to Virgil and Theocritus. Just using the Idylls title allows one to mute the harsher realities of country life—the celibacy, cruelties, injustices, ignorance. It also allows you to keep history at arm's length without actually denying its force. To return to your earlier question about time, I guess I was aiming at 'a time aside from time', a prose that preserved the texture of a lived-in place but shifted it into a dimension that belongs to the memory—where it was purified and clarified by the fact it was no more. A book that helped was Calvino's *Invisible Cities*, partly because it's both colloquial and formulaic. Stunningly inventive, too, which I couldn't emulate—but I kept in play a notion of the farm as itself an invisible city. But in the end the lenses are irrelevant. It's only what you see, and hear, that counts. My hope would be that the Idylls, and indeed *The Holy Land* overall , is 'a read' that has a recognizable complete effect.

There's something going on with golf here too, isn't there? The sequence 'Idylls', in 18 sections, is the centrepiece of a collection entitled The Holy Land. How schematic is the absence of the first person from the sequence?

Well, I have wondered in my own mind if Dante didn't invent golf in the *Inferno*! With the pair of them, golfer and caddie, playing their way around each tricky episode towards an outcome—and then just as one encounter ends the next comes into view. And it's true the farm has 18 fields, so it seems set up to be a golf course. You might suspect it's all a Simpsons' version of the *Purgatorio*! So I suppose what you have spotted there is a vein of humour.

I hadn't thought at all about the absent first person, other than to follow an eavesdropping and, as I imagined it, an implied child observer, who then in the last 18th idyll—at least in my mind—speaks up. So the spell of that childhood world is broken and thereafter, in the verse poems, you have an actual father-son dialogue. But that only occurs to me now in response to your question.

It is a schematic book. But although that's true, it's not that significant. Poetry is schematic, formulaic, the way several stanzas of a poem will keep to a rhyme pattern. But the formula isn't truly mathematical, it doesn't have a binding further significance. It's more like the way a hand of poker can have a pattern and so have a value within the rules of the game. That kind of arranging and sorting allows one to fool around. My hope though was that the overall effect was robust. I don't mind at all if people read it straight, as autobiography, as indeed they do: what it was like to grow up on a farm in East Cork 50 years ago. Even so, I'd be surprised if there weren't some twinklings and ticklings in the impression it leaves on them.

'Understorey' seems to echo Yeats's 'Cuchulainn Comforted' and the loose terza rima section at the end of 'Little Gidding' where Eliot appears to encounter the ghost of Yeats. How conscious or deliberate are these echoes? It's a deceptively formal book: ending with the villanelle 'The January Birds'.

I hadn't thought of 'Cuchullain Comforted', though I can see now why you would. Yikes, that whole ending section is courting, or skirting, literary cliché ... Yeats, Eliot, Heaney. Looking at it now from a distance, I can see that. At the time I just needed, in that particular section, to write some lines about the birth of my children. (It's not to compare like to like, but Borges said Dante wrote his whole poem so he could imagine meeting Beatrice once more—surely the most poignant observation.) Obviously I hoped then, and do now, that a reader is carried through the episode on a fair wind with the help of my rough-and-ready terza rima.

'The January Birds' is I suppose more observant of form. In terms of the—by now—rather obvious schema, it brings us out of winter and returns us to the upper world. I wrote the poem one of those warm winters in London when blackbirds and thrushes sang through the winter. What's one to make of that? Birds singing, cheerfully but out-of-season.

In the three uncollected poems included, two return to that homeplace. Does every poet have subject matter you can never get away from? 'Stars and Jasmine', which is not about the farm you grew up on, is a real cracker.

I suspect we all do have some 'place' we return to, where we first experienced perhaps both the shock and pleasure of language, the original excitement of utterance. But I don't think it has to be an actual location. It might be a time of day, a house, certain conditions of light or weather. Lisgoold, childhood, the farm, are obviously at the centre of *The Holy Land*, but they are re-imagined and quite different to a factual recreation. And other settings—English, urban, North-American or purely imagined places—turn up in my poems. I think poems develop their own dynamic. The best analogy might be a serial dream, which distorts one's recognizable world and yet has some sort of continuity. Poems are like that. You can't say where they might take you next. And at their best they take one to the unexpected.

I'm glad you're keen on 'Stars and Jasmine'. It's not such a new poem but one of a couple left orphaned by *The Holy Land*. Its setting is our old London place. The anecdote of the cat, the hedgehog, and the tortoise is true—or true-ish. So that's a reminder that the world can come up with the poems. One needn't do much then, except pay attention and follow a few rules. If you're lucky. But talking about one's poems too much may be bad luck—especially the new stuff. It makes me nervous. It's too much like walking on soft cement.

TIME OUT

Such is modern life STEPHEN DOBYNS

The two young ones fed, bathèd, zippered, read to and sung to. Asleep.
Time now to stretch on the sofa. Time for a cigarette.
When he realizes he's out. Clean out of smokes.
He grabs a fistful of coins, hesitates to listen before
Pulling the door softly to. Then sprints for the cornershop.

When he trips on a shoelace, head first into the path of a U-turning cab.
The screech of brakes is coterminous with his scream.
The Somalian shopkeeper, who summons the ambulance, knows the
    face,
But the name or address? No—just someone he remembers
Popping in, always with kids (this he doesn't say).

Casualty is at full stretch and the white thirtyish male,
Unshaven, with broken runners, is going nowhere. Is cleanly dead.
Around midnight an orderly rummages his pockets: £2.50 in change,
A latchkey, two chestnuts, one mitten, scraps of paper,
Some written on, but no wallet, cards, licence, or address book.

Around 2 a.m. he's put on ice, with a numbered tag.
Around 3 a.m. a child wakes, cries, then wails for attention.
But after ten minutes, unusually, goes back to sleep.
Unusually his twin sleeps on undisturbed till six o'clock,
When they both wake together, kicking, calling out *dada, dada*

Happily: well slept, still dry, crooning and pretend-reading in the
    half-light.
Then one slides to the floor, toddles to the master bedroom
And, seeing the empty (unmade) bed, toddles towards the stairs,
Now followed by the other, less stable, who stumbles halfway down
And both roll the last five steps to the bottom, screaming.

To be distracted by the post plopping onto the mat: all junk,
Therefore bulky, colourful, glossy, illicit. Time slips.
Nine o'clock: hungry, soiled, sensing oddness and absence,
Edgy together and whimpering now, when they discover the TV
Still on, its 17-channel console alive to their touch.

The Italian Parliament, sumo wrestling, the Austrian Grand Prix,
Opera, the Parcel Force ad, see them through to half past nine
When distress takes hold and the solid stereophonic screaming begins,
Relentless and shrill enough to penetrate the attention
Of the retired French pharmacist next door

Who at, say ten o'clock, pokes a broomstick through her rear window
To rattle theirs: magical silencing effect, lasting just so long
As it takes for the elderly woman to draw up her shopping list,
To retrieve two tenners from the ice-compartment, deadlock her front
    doors,
Shake her head at the sunning milk, and make it to the bus.

Let us jump then to 10 p.m., to the nightmare dénouement . . .
No, let us duck right now out of this story, for such it is:
An idle, day-bed, Hitchcockian fantasy (though prompted by a news
    item,

A clockwork scenario: it was five days before that three-year-old
Was discovered beside the corpse of his Irish dad in Northolt).

Let us get *this* dad in and out of the shop, safely across the street,
Safely indoors again, less a couple of quid, plus the listings mags
And ten Silk Cut, back on board the sofa: reprieved, released, relaxed,
Thinking it's time for new sneakers, for a beard trim, for an overall
Rethink in the hair department. Time maybe to move on from the fags.

RURAL ELECTRIFICATION 1956

We woke to the clink of crowbars
and the smell of creosote along the road.
Stripped to his britches, our pole-man
tossed up red dirt as we watched him
sink past his knees, past his navel:
Another day, he called out to us,
and I'll be through to Australia . . .
Later we brought him a whiskey bottle
tucked inside a Wellington sock and filled
with tea. He sat on the verge and told
of years in London, how he'd come home,
more fool, to share in the good times;
and went on to describe AC/DC, ohms,
insulation, potential difference,
so that the lights of Piccadilly
were swaying among the lamps of fuchsia,
before he disappeared into the earth.

INDIAN SUMMER

On the last afternoon
of my first visit

to London, I struck off
into the thick of Oxford Street,

where I bought, at Debenham's,
an imitation leopard-skin

suit (too tight) for my girlfriend
and a chocolate-brown

cord blazer (too large) for myself,
then turned the corner

onto the Edgware Road
to my ultimate destination,

Ann Summers' Sex Shop
(the original one, I believe)

where I bought an assortment
of condoms and a magazine

from the Lady herself,
who jingled her earrings

as she handed over
my purchases, saying

It must be gorgeous! Ireland,
the countryside, in this heat.

LONG DISTANCE

So, for a season, he lived within
earshot of the railroads, in a room
furnished with sofabed, table, lamp,
silent fridge, a telephone.
At night he heard the freight trains
roll endlessly across the heartland.
They kept him up, sometimes till dawn,
beside a green radio and a map,
where he tracked the same baseball scores,
rapes, fires and murders, and much
the same humidity and heat
from the Lakes to the Gulf.
Once he dialled a number long distance.
Six, seven, eight times it rang.
No answer. He shifted the handset
to his chest, letting it ring and ring.

LAST CALL

Home late, his house asleep, a man goes to the phone,
and from habit, expecting nothing, touches the Recall.
But this time he tenses to hear the electronic scramble,
the pause before the lottery digits fall into place.
At the other end, sure enough, he hears a male voice,
no one he recognizes, repeating *Hello, hello?*
He can hear background piano, Chopin or John Field,
establishing a room, smoke-filled, larger than his,
where wine in a discarded glass is losing its chill,
while the voice continues, good-humoured, persuasive:
Come on, say something. He tries to picture a face, a hand,
to fit the voice, still in his ear, still going on, *Last chance…*
He hangs up, his own hand shaking with intimacy.

MILK

This notebook in which he used to sketch
has, on its expensive-looking black cover,

a sprinkle of whitish stains: of the sort
sure to detain the unborn biographer.

Could they be the miniaturist's impression
of the northern sky, his Starry Night?

Or might lab-tests point to something else?
That they are, in fact, human milk-stains,

the effect of lactic acid on cheap skin,
and date from five years earlier—

a time when his wife's hyperactive glands
used to lob milk right across the room

to the wing-chair in which he dozed,
the sketchbook (it seems) closed in his hands.

Though he felt its light lash on his skin
many a night, he never took to that milk

and wished only for a wider room.
A failure of imagination, you might claim,

though it could be he needed more
of human kindness from that source then.

You could even say that the milk stopped,
but the acid didn't. That he replied in kind.

And thus it began: the pointless unstoppable game
across a room, in which a child grew

less small, and became the mesmerized umpire
looking now one way, now the other.

SOME SPORTING MOTIFS

The ball-games of the north-western tribes
have their origins in the spoils of war.
The ball at your feet is the trophy,
the head of the enemy you have slain
being booted homewards through the fields
or passed along the line of warriors,
after the glorious summer campaign.

As for games with sticks—such as shinty,
hurling, hockey, golf—you must compare
the design of the modern cricket-ball
with its analogue, the Irish *sliotar*:
two 'eights' of dried skin, hemp-sewn around
a light, bouncey core. *Balls* it could be called,
or *bollocks*, to indicate its dual number;

while the stick itself is a surrogate,
toy sword—for this was the pastime
of the camp-followers: the boys and women.
Hence, the spectacle of camogie.
Hence, indeed, the sphere of harness leather
patched around a core of whiskey corks,
sewn and re-sewn, by my mother.

A WORD FROM THE LOKI

The Loki tongue does not lend itself
to description along classical lines.
Consider the vowels: there are just four,
including one produced by inspiration
(i.e. indrawn breath), which then requires
an acrobatic feat of projection
to engage with its troupe of consonants.
The skilled linguist can manage, at best,
a sort of tattoo; whereas the Loki
form sounds of balletic exactness.
Consider further: that the tribe has evolved
this strenuous means of articulation
for one word, a defective verb
used in one mood only, the optative.

No semantic equivalent can be found
in English, nor within Indo-European.
Loosely, the word might be glossed as *to joke*,
provided we cite several other usages,
such as *to recover from snakebite*;
to eat fish with the ancestors;
*to die at home in the village, survived
by all of one's sons and grandsons.*
It is prohibited in daily speech,
and the Loki, a moderate people
who abjure physical punishments,
are severe in enforcing this taboo,
since all offenders, of whatever age
or status, are handed over to *mouri*

—sent, in effect, to a gruesome death:
for the victim is put on board a raft,
given a gourd of drinking water, a knife,
and one of those raucous owl-faced
monkeys as companion, then towed
to midstream and set loose on the current.
Yet the taboo is relaxed at so-called
'joke parties': impromptu celebrations
that can be provoked by multiple births
or by an out-of-season catch of bluefish.
They are occasions for story-telling
and poetry, and serve a useful end
in allowing the young to learn this verb
and to perfect its exact delivery.

For the word is held to have come down
from the ancestral gods, to be their one gift.
And its occult use is specific: to ward off
the Loordhu, a cannibalistic horde,
believed to roam the interior forest,
who are reputed to like their meat
fresh and raw, to keep children in lieu of pigs,
and to treat eye and tongue as delicacies.
The proximity of danger is heralded
by a despondency that seems to strike
without visible cause but which effects
a swift change among a people by nature
brave and practical, bringing to a stop
in a matter of hours all work, play, talk.

At such crises, the villagers advance
to the riverbank and, as night falls,
they climb into the trees, there to recite
this verb throughout the hours of darkness.
But since, in the memory of the village,
the Loordhu have never yet attacked,
one has reason to doubt the existence
of an imminent threat to the Loki—
who nonetheless continue, in suspense, their chant.
At once wistful and eerie, it produces
this observable result: that it quells
the commotion of the guenon monkeys
and lulls, within its range, the great forest.

THE SLOE

That he died alone in the gully
below the pass in a snowstorm, the first
of the year, in a lurch of the seasons
which became a change of climate;
that he died some three to five weeks
after an assault—from a wild beast
or fellow man—which shattered
his ribcage and sent him above
the tree-line, far from the settlements,
that he died really from
being alone, an injured man
relying on his few resources—which were,
however, both innate and military,

so that he carried about him
not only weapons and tools
but spares, medicine, and a sewing kit,
fire, and the means of fire,
and was observant and skilled
about stone, wood, grasses, skins,
about stag-horn and bone—knew for each
its properties and use, but he died
like Xenophon's comrades on the trek
home through Armenia, as soldiers
have died on all recorded
winter marches, not from lack of discipline
or the body's weakness, or not only,
but because of the slight
shortening of the odds which comes
with the unexpected comfort of snow;
so that prepared for the next day's climb,
his equipment in order,
the backpack, the axe, the two
birch-bark containers, one holding
tinder and flints, the other
insulated with damp sycamore leaves
(but no longer carrying live embers),
the quiver, and beside it the straight new bow
with its unused string, the bird net
spread, the pannier upright,
he ate the last of his food
—all except, oddly, a sloe—
then lay on his uninjured side
in the best available shelter

and pillowed his head, while the snow
(which would lull and warm him)
spiralled out of the night and marked,
as I've said, a change in the Tyrol,
a climatic glitch which lasted 5,000 years
until the thaw on the glacier two summers ago
brought him to our attention,
then here to the Institute;
so that, although I can tell you
nothing of his gods or language,
almost nothing of his way of life,
whether he was shepherd, headman,
or shaman, the last of his village
or employed on some delicate embassy;
whether he moved in the forest
among spirits and shades
or was himself almost a shadow
who with a visceral roar
fell on a victim and bludgeoned
his brains, whether on a raid
he would satisfy his need with a woman or child
or, contrariwise, was himself
husband and father,
a tender of flocks in the epoch
of transhumance: gregarious, hierarchical,
a transmitter of geographical lore,
of trails, cloud changes, windbreaks,
who sang at the camp fire—
though I can tell you nothing of this
I can tell exactly

how he died, how in his plight
he couldn't string the green yew stave,
he couldn't ignite the tinder
to roast the songbirds
and, from the decalcified traces
on the humerus, I can tell
he kept, those last weeks, one arm
crooked, in a virtual sling,
thus giving the broken ribs time
to knit (as indeed they were doing)
and can guess, in the interim, he hoped
for an Indian summer of nuts, mushrooms, fruit,
a fire not quite dead,
even a maggot-ridden carcass;
and for a hand with the bow stave
he would have given in exchange his knife
or his coloured tassel with its marble bead,
that one inutile item polished
so spherical and white
it seems, like the sloe,
extraneous . . . but everything
comes down to the sloe, the uneaten sloe:
herders from Anatolia to the Ötzal,
even to the present day, pick
these sour, purplish almost pith-less fruits
and, like my Grandfather Bögelmann
when he dropped one in his fob,
they say 'A frost will sweeten it'
—so it is grave goods, viaticum
food for the soul on its journey,

in its flight from the tip
of the punctured heel or the slit
tattooed into the lumbar,
and when the temperature drops
and the body's anaesthetized,
as the brain sinks into its reverie
of log fires and song,
of dripping fat and tree sap,
even as the skin adheres to the earth,
the tannins and acids disintegrate
so that now, as I put the sloe back in the ice,
I tell you it is edible,
that, by morning, it was sweet.

FROST

after Seán Ó'Ríordáin

I found a hankie on the whitethorn
outside in the freezing cold this morning.
When I reached up to get it, it slipped—
or skipped? Anyhow it missed my grip.
Not just a sprightly rag, I thought,
more like 'something' died out here last night . . .
As I sought the right analogy
this surfaced in my memory:
    The kiss I gave my cousin
    before they covered her coffin.

SILK

Should I tell you that just a century ago,
in the year of my father's—your granddad's—birth
the distribution of the silk industry
stretched as far as Tiverton to the west
and north to the looms and tenements of Paisley,

or that when, technically, silk is *thrown*
a single filament which is drawn unbroken
from the cocoon can measure a kilometre or more
and so, in this, it shares a subtle topology
with the network of veins beneath the skin,

which when stretched across, say, your collar—
or your pelvic-bone will reveal the bluish hues
of *Bombyx mori* eggs when they're freshly laid;
and since your skin has something too of the texture,
even the smell, of shantung and raw tussore

must I not then repeat to you the words of Count
Dandolo who, in his treatise on sericulture,
wrote of the worm itself: 'the greater the heat
in which it is hatched, the greater are its wants,
the more rapid its pleasures, the shorter its existence'?

ON NOT EXPERIENCING THE
ULTRAVIOLET CATASTROPHE

Unlike my childhood neighbour Jacksy Hickey
Who, rain or shine, wore a black gabardine,

Reasoning what was good to keep heat in
Was good enough, by definition, to keep it out,

We, when we reach the heart of the cornfield,
Know better: we shed each other's clothes.

Oh, you are radiant, my dear, and I am hot for thee!
But what, you ask, is heat? This I claim to know . . .

Then I tell you why a tea cup doesn't scorch
And why, for instance, Josiah Wedgwood's kilns

Only baked Black Country clays to lucent jasper
With the help of an unknown hand: the constant h

Blocking frequencies in the ultraviolet range
And which, according to our century's laws,

Is true even to the cosmic radiation coming
At us, year on year, from the origins of time.

A modest number, with its dairy herd of noughts
After the point, it almost is—but isn't—zero.

By its mercy, we lie in the face of heaven.
You may lie beside me flesh to flesh. For this

You may be shunned, you may turn a dusky porcelain.
My love, you may be skinned. But you will not burn.

THE WINEGLASS

We can never play it back again,
Our love-life's little song and story.
The wineglass slips your fingers' hold
And signals to the planet's core.
I could, for just one millisecond,
Restore the moment to your hand.
Instead we watch it gather force
Along the curve-line through the floor.
We can never play it back again,
Our love-life's little song and story.

SOUTHPAW

I'm surprised, you could say a little shocked,
to find your left hand equals mine
now we're landed in this heat-struck Welsh stubble
we've jumped several hundred miles to

and it's either a split second or several months
since, on the splintering boards of your flat,

you were feeding me half-pint mickeys
of aquavit in ice-cold sips from your mouth.

You push and I ache but I hold you steady.
And I've time now to take in the boy's shoulders,
the mannish cut of the jaw, the hairline
of sweat above the lip and the metis-brown

all-over burn of your skin, time and world enough,
before we either bite or kiss, to overhear
—is it Mammy's voice from beyond the grave?—
That one, she could do with a scrub, son.

THE DINNER CALL

in memory

My mother comes to the doorstep
and issues her dinner call: three rising notes,
something between a yodel and a mimicked cockcrow.
I rise from the sand-heap. And I listen.
She questions me with one cupped ear.
Did we hear it, or not? A faint answering *halloo.*

My mother comes to the doorstep,
her head back, one hand shading her slant eyes,
and issues her dinner call: a sound I can hear
but cannot quite repeat—not a shout, nor yet song,
but carrying to the summery-silent fields,
to the Glens, to the Big Bog, and the Little Bog;

to my father birthing a calf; to the men
stooking barley or winding hay; to the sowers,
the reapers and the binders; to hire and help,
the vets and pole-men and drainage inspectors;
to the old dray Jack, and Billy the wild one;
to girls out blackberrying; the boys naked
in the stream; her brothers coursing a hare;
to the quiet man fencing the boundary;
to my namesake, and to my son's namesake;
to her own father ploughing the Back Field.

My mother comes to the doorstep
and issues her dinner call: three rising notes.
And the voice carries and holds.

from **THE IDYLLS**

2

Another day when they were sitting on the headland in the Small
Fields, the men discussed the changes they had seen and a debate
arose about what was the greatest change had happened in their life-
time.

'What do you think?' My father asked Dan-Jo.

'The steam tractor was a great change,' the trucker answered. 'And
then the motor car. But the greatest of all to my mind was the cutter-
and-binder.'

'That was a great change,' my father said. 'And you, Alf, what would
you say?'

'When the dam was built at Ardnacrusha it flooded farmland in
seven parishes,' said the Gully.

'Yes, that was a great and a terrible change,' my father agreed. 'Moss, you've seen more than any of us. What's your opinion?'

'Women's fashion,' the forester replied. 'Girls these days in next to nothing at Mass.'

My father nodded, 'That too is a great change.' And the rest chipped in and everyone had a different opinion about what was the greatest change in their lifetime: television, the creamery, penicillin, Shannon airport, the price of stout, false teeth, tourists, the electric fence, plastic bags, weedkiller.

'There are a lot of changes,' my father said.

Moss turned to him, 'Tell us, Martin, what you think.'

My father fished in his inside pocket and took out a small framed photo of a woman in a wide hat and veil, smiling happily.

'That,' he said, 'is my mother on her honeymoon.'

9

It was only mud, my father said. Nothing but muck and mud.

He had stormed into the house and was threatening to sell the farm. He was putting it under the hammer, he said. It no longer afforded any sort of life. And who had he to pass it on to? No one knew where the bounds' ditch was. No one but himself and maybe the dog. They mightn't credit him but the For Sale sign was going up. He'd met a man in Fermoy who wanted to buy the whole shagging lot for a golf course.

My mother said why didn't he sell to him then, and to shut up about it.

But Moss said 'twas only the whiskey talking. In the morning he'd have forgotten about it. And they would be out in the fields the same as always.

'It's a mystery where he's gone.'

It was the morning after dragging the river. Young Hyland had been fishing for trout with onion bags and had drowned in a pool. The men had worked through the night by the light of storm lamps. But the body hadn't been recovered. They had come home to see to the cows and were drinking whiskey in the Old House while their clothes dried before the fire.

'It's a mystery how it happened in the first place.'

'They said when he went under he never came to the surface again, though they thought they heard him call three times.'

'His foot must have been caught by a root.'

'Maybe he was pulled down by a current or a whirlpool.'

'It's not as if this is the Blackwater.'

'They say it takes three lives a year,' said Davey Divine.

'The bodies often turn up miles downstream or are washed in from the ocean months after.'

'I wouldn't want to be the one to come upon them then,' said Moss.

'Still they say it's not the worst way to go.'

'I always drown the kittens and pups,' said Jo. 'Better that than stringing them from the clothes-line.'

'Or feeding them to the sow, like the Gully does.'

'I think it must be frightening to die under the water.'

'Why do you think that, 'Son?'

'Because how would you be able to say the Act of Contrition?'

The men laughed, 'Maybe you should keep away from those Coakley sisters.'

My father said, 'I think, 'Son, it would be enough to repeat the words in your head.'

17

'Does the apple let go of the tree—or does the tree give it a nudge?'

We were in the Orchard gathering the windfalls before school. St Martin's Summer, the frost turning to dew or the dew already becoming frost. Unbroken spider webs joined branch to branch and tree to tree, the Bramleys to the Pippins, the Golden Russets to the Blenheim Oranges, the crab apple to our ancient Calville Blank Diver.

So: does the fledgling take wing or do the parent birds push it from the nest? Does the soul abandon the body or the body with its last strength send it on its way? Does the Father beget the Son, or is the Son one with the Father? Do the living replace the dead or do the dead souls hinder the living? Does the hand cast the stone? Or does the stone wriggle from the hand? We were in the Orchard gathering windfalls. We filled our caps and aprons, though there was no wind that year.

18

Davey, the Bo'son and myself were with my father topping beet in Buckleys' Field. We pulled the muddy tubers out of the ground, trimmed the roots with the blade, then sliced off the green heads and tossed the finished beet into a wicker barrow. A north-east wind was blowing down from the Galtees and sending black squalls of rain and sleet across the open country.

The light faded and my father proposed a halt. We stood together in the lee of the beech.

'It's no beauty spot, the dead end of October.'

'On fine nights,' my father said, 'Moss used to lie out on the old lime kiln under the stars. One time he nodded off and he damn near finished up in the kiln.'

The Bo'son said he liked lying on the Haggard wall after supper and listening to the wind in the pines. 'The air in the Haggard is soft, almost like a woman's breath.'

'You can't ever have been in the van with Éil Dade then.'

But Davey said he preferred company, even if it was only someone to argue with. Oftentimes now he sat by the well and played a tune on the whistle. 'Just to myself and the hound.'

'And what about you, Boss, who knows every rood of the land. What is your favourite haunt?'

My father said it was Colman's Glen. 'Where the sloe bush straddles the stream. And there's never a soul, only the birds. That's the place I'll be spending my holidays.'

MEDIUMS

Acts 2:13

He drank only *mejums* on his outings
to marts, funerals, race meetings.
After a few he'd break into song.
A few more and he spoke in tongues.

*

My father hops across nimble as a piebald pony,
then lifts the single strand of electrified wire
for myself to follow after.

We're on a mission to retrieve a heifer
out of Keegan's sugar beet, but have detoured
by way of Lesseps and the Parc Guell.

A white-faced Hereford, who's made daylight
of Keegan's ditch to find somewhat more to her liking
than our green-and-gold strip

of furze and ragwort, more in keeping with her forebears,
maybe, on the Welsh marches—or has she smelled
the strawberry fields of Tibidabo?

My father lifts the strand of rusted wire,
careful it won't snag on the T-shirt
I bought this morning on the Ramblas.

Even so, it shows all the wilfulness
of the pup Goldfinger on a leash,
or a mountain hare drawn by Miro,

and whips back to catch the *e* of *libre*
smack in the eye, drawing blood
from the apostolic face of Che Guevara.

UNDERSTOREY

A shoal of starlings lifts and skims the bounds
at our approach. Beyond, in the muddy stubble,
plover and lapwing graze between the cows.

They can't see me. He shakes his blackthorn
in anger—or in greeting? *See, they can't see me!*
He laughs. 'It means I'll not live to see them born.'

We've come to the Bottom Glen, where the stream
goes under alder and bog myrtle, then drops
through barbs of rusty furze to Dillon's field.

'This is where the souls of all our line await
their hour of coming hither. And those two
in the crowd—the one so shy she hides her face

in hair and hardly dares to look your way,
and that other with the game leg whose sight
is dimmed but whose gaze is bared to heaven,

his forehead flaming like some young colt's—
they will be yours, your lot. You, once scorched
by their souls' twin-flame, will seek your destiny.

But you'll need courage then to untie your tongue,
strength too in the face of ignominy and insult.
Should you succeed, it will be due to them.

We've come to the end. Look over your shoulder
—but not towards the house—and you'll find
we have erased each field even as we walked.

The way ahead is over water, the way back
through landfill, rubble, roundabouts and raw estates
—Finnsgrove, Meadowvale, Elsinore Heights.

Streets where once were fields like those I tilled,
with foreign makes of car parked up drives
where mares in foal have stood, and men with pikes.

And the Bucks' Gate where the Tans one night stalled
their Crossley Tender—they didn't come within
but swore and relieved themselves against our wall—

you'll find it's bulldozed wide, our old passage
now once more a public right of way for folk
I've not met and have no wish to meet.

I never dealt in life with a man or woman whose name
I didn't know, whose kin I had not followed
or shouldered to their plot of consecrated ground.

But you belong to different times, you who are the age
I was the day you were born. By then I was too old
for all this, and now I've nothing more to give.

Do not flinch. Is not that the outside light come on
in Colman's yard? I should better go. But here,
take my old coat, and this my beaten hat for headgear.'

With that he swung his compact frame about and went,
nearby that stunted bush with its stringy beard of catkin.
His words with birdcalls mingled in the pissing rain.

THE JANUARY BIRDS

The birds in Nunhead Cemetery begin
Before I've flicked a switch, turned on the gas.
There must be some advantage to the light

I tell myself, viewing my slackened chin
Mirrored in the rain-dark window glass,
While from the graveyard's trees, the birds begin.

An image from a dream survives the night,
Some dreck my head refuses to encompass.
There must be some advantage to the light.

You are you I mouth to my shadow skin,
Though you are me, assuming weight and mass—
While from the graveyard's trees, the birds begin:

Thrush, blackbird, finch—then rooks take fright
At a skip-truck and protest, cawing en masse.
There must be some advantage to the light

Or birds would need the gift of second sight
To sing *Another year will come to pass!*
The birds in Nunhead Cemetery begin,
There must be some advantage to the light.

THE DUN COW

What's the Dun Cow doing in the Old Kent Road,
I'm wondering, when who should blow in
But this boyo wearing the moss-green gabardine
My mother wore when out feeding the hens.

Those beaks were taking it in turns to coax
Crushed oats from between her toes, her horny
Old toes covered over with sores, with the bunions
and warts that stuck out through her brogues.

So how're they keeping? There's rheum in his eye.
I had truck with them all—all the old crowd.
Yer da and yer ma, and the man in Dungourney?

Tucked up with their rosaries, they are,
Piled one on the other at home in Lisgoold,
Pushing up daisies for many the long year.

STARS AND JASMINE

Each of them has been a god many times:
cat, hedgehog and—our summer interloper—the tortoise.
A perfect triangle, they can neither eat
nor marry one another.
And tonight they are gods
under the jasmine under the stars.

Already the hedgehog has scoffed the cat's supper
and she's walked nonplussed beside him
escaping headlong into the bushes.
Wisely now, she keeps an eye on him there,
and on the tortoise
noisily criss-crossing the gravel.

For the cat, jasmine is white
but the stars have colours.
For the hedgehog, there are no stars
only a sky of jasmine,
against which he sniffs something dark,
outlined like a bird of prey.

Wisely, the tortoise ignores both jasmine and stars.
Isn't it enough, she says, to carry the sky on your back,
a sky that is solid, mathematical and delicately coloured—
on which someone, too, has painted
our neighbours' address: 9a Surrey Rd.
Come September, we will lower her through their letterbox.

THE NESTS

for Kathryn

You ask again about the nests—the wren's
housed in the ivy above the broken pier,
a goldcrest's low in the privet,
the robin's safe in the clump of pampas.
And below the Lane Gate coal tits
have built in the hollow post.
If you run your hand up the damp shaft
you'll find the spot, where the metal is warm.
They lead us away from the yard,
under the barbed wire and down the lane to the Long Field.
We'll keep in the lee of the ditch for shelter.

Overhead a mistle-thrush stirs the hawthorn,
as out in the wind the larks have settled
in cups of grass-corn for the night.
When we cross to the Glen a snipe catapults
from the rushes close by your feet.
Now we approach the wall-dark of the wood
hearing within the wounded call of an owlet.
We come in due course to a river, where I lie face down
on your surface, the rain soft on my spine.

Gerard Fanning

By way of background, what is the earliest poem in this selection? Can you remember when and where it was written, and in what spirit? More particularly, what do you recall of Ireland and its poetry at the moment of composition, and of how you defined your creative ambitions starting out?

'Waiting on Lemass'. It was written in my parents' house in Dublin in the early 1970s. I had published some poems in undergraduate magazines and broadsheets (do they exist anymore?) and was trying to finish work to send to David Marcus' New Irish Writing page in The Irish Press. As was his impeccable style, he replied immediately and his encouragement was the spur I needed.

In those days there were independent bookshops (do they exist anymore?)—the Eblana, Parson's, Fred Hanna—which stocked and stacked high, publications from small poetry presses. The Dolmen Press accepted occasional first collections but was in decline and though Thomas Kinsella had left for America, Austin Clarke could still be seen in the bookshops around Grafton Street. Seamus Heaney's and Derek Mahon's first books had appeared and further afield the major influences (do they exist anymore?) were Bishop, Gunn, Larkin and Lowell.

Early 70s was definitely a different Ireland and many of your landscapes in Easter Snow seem to pre-date 1992, the year of publication. 'Waiting on Lemass', for example, maps the exquisite tedium of a childhood in 1960s Ireland. If the earliest poem was early 1970s, and your first book appeared in 1992, it must have felt as if several collections were compressed into one?

Exactly. And too much freight added, at times. 'Waiting on Lemass' deliberately confused Sean Lemass and Alex Leamas, the main character in Le Carré's *The Spy who Came in from the Cold*. The film version was made in Smithfield in Dublin. They needed a cheap location that resembled bombed-out Berlin. It was made in grainy black & white (what great colors they are) with Richard Burton and Claire Bloom—real exotica in Dublin at that time, Burton and Liz Taylor downing pints in local bars. The tedium you mention was real but only in a 50s and 60s childhood sense, where church and state had genuine control. By the mid to late 60s that seemed like so much froth and everything was possible.

By the late 70s, most of my contemporaries seemed to know exactly what to do about getting a book deal but my output was always an issue. As soon as I gathered 25-30 poems together I would start deleting them in fives and sixes as not suitable, and so never seemed to reach the required figure to interest a publisher. In short, a lot was discarded, a lot compressed. It finally got to the stage in 1990-91 that friends were losing patience and encouraged me to send something to John Deane at Dedalus Press and he agreed to publish *Easter Snow* in 1992. I'm not sure what ambition I had for the book, but it was very kindly received.

Speaking of Le Carré, several of the poems in Easter Snow adopt the grammar and drama of superior spy novels and film noir; the man alone and nameless and working under cover. Le Carré, Graham Greene, John Buchan . . . Can you say something of what attracts you to this figure and how it adapts to poetry?

More likely film noir. I like the confused look of 'the not too bright' private eye. Or just confusion, wrong man, wrong place—Greene's *Our Man in Havana*. In the TV version of *Tinker, Tailor, Soldier, Spy* the civil service mentality was amusing, that dull quotidian stuff. Nearer the mark might be Mahon's 'Last of the Fire Kings'—'the man / Who drops at night / From a moving train / And strikes out over the fields / Where fireflies glow, / Not knowing a word of the language.' Making it up as you go along.

From what you're saying, you seem to get some kind of imaginative buzz out of that persona of nameless faceless civil servant. Is this fair? Your second book is Working for the Government. *A lot of poets never write about their real jobs. There is a definite tradition of Irish poets who worked on behalf of the state: Denis Devlin, Dennis O'Driscoll... Are your colleagues aware of your other life? Or is poetry a version of secrecy, of being under cover, for you? In purely practical terms, how does the poetry fit into the life of a civil servant? And how does that work translate poetry?*

The faceless civil servant might be a little too Kafkaesque—but there is a permanent government or class who wield power and say nothing. Having a job gives me the prosaic cash to just get on with things. And so, for now, it's the 'in tray' as 'the lights come on at four, at the end of another year.' The 'Working for the Government' title was a nod to Talking Heads ('Don't Worry About The Government'). I have never worked 9–5. The job is outdoors, which involves visiting businesses, interviewing and field work. It's a bit like a benign *Glengarry Glen Ross*, sharing anecdotes with colleagues; when I'm back, writing up in the office. This freedom has a Maverick quality, with all the foolishness that entails. Eccentricities such as poetry are easily accommodated. If there is a covert, subversive quality to the other life of poetry, you do it in your head, on the bus, observing all the time. The job stuff is a progression from 'Toads' to 'Toads Revisited' and no harm in that.

Apart from those you mention, there were poets such as Valintin Iremonger and Richard Ryan (who I met a few times) in the diplomatic corps. No doubt, they too grabbed the time for writing regardless of how the crust was earned.

The density of reference in some of the second book's poems might baffle some Amer-
ican readers. Can you describe the peripheral landscape of 'July in Bettystown', and
say, perhaps, what the ever-present sea represents in your imagination? In 'The Fifties
Parent' the image of your father is conflated with that of Nikita Khrushchev. Is there
a Cold War sensibility in your work, where provincial life is loomed over by super pow-
ers, as in Muldoon's 'Cuba'? I suppose I hear it too in, again, the Fleming reference.

I've always lived beside the sea. Here in Dublin, and all childhood hol-
idays twenty-five miles or so north of Dublin, where we rented my
aunt's house each July in Bettystown. At that time, Bettystown was lit-
tle more than a string of summer houses, a bump in the road, but it
had a few shops and a hotel, and for me, a certain naive Rockwell qual-
ity. My older brothers were beginning to drift off to London etc. So
the rest of us spent every day on the beach, swimming, making dams,
smoking, the usual ten-year-old stuff. We seemed to be living as in-
significant dots, while the real glamour was starting to relay back
from my brothers settling in to London. Later at UCD I realized Ro-
nan Sheehan and Neil Jordan were writing their first fictions about
the same area.

The impressions laid down in those years, the color and smell of
the sea and the sky, barley fields stretching back from the dunes, horse
racing on the strand, are like something from Alain-Fournier's Le
Grand Meaulnes. All gone now, of course. This was the time of Ken-
nedy's White House and Khrushchev's Bond villain. And my bald fa-
ther hovering, smiling and seeming to say 'everything will be all
right'. If I was too young to understand the Cold War, it did pervade
the times, even in sleepy Bettystown.

What is 'Murphy's Hexagon' that it should merit a revisit? The tidal nature of Omey
seems to make the sea, in this poem at least, an ever-present symbol of inevitability

and chance. Wasn't MacNeice's father partly reared on Omey? Also, can you say something about the form: the long lines and the couplets and the series of rhetorical questions?

I was with a group in the early 70s that included Patrick King. He was starting to publish poems and knew Richard Murphy. I had just got a car and we decided on a whim to drive over to the west of Ireland. Murphy had a slight mania for boats, Galway Hookers and the like and building and doing up houses. He writes about it in his collection *The Price of Stone*. We heard he had built a small one-roomed house in the shape of a hexagon on Omey Island. So we drove across, looked in the window and there he was reading. He invited us in for a cup of tea and gave us each a neat signed edition of *High Island: Selected Poems*, from Harper & Row. You can only drive across twice a day, so I was keen not to miss the tide. The revisit was after King's early death, the house had been sold, and the more mundane domestic look of the place was the usual disappointment. There is a MacNeice connection on his father's side. As for the form, long lines seemed to suit the meandering jour-neys.

'Leaving St Helens' and 'Quinsy' ... Can you say something about the density of allusion in each of those two poems?

To misquote Larkin, 'illness is no different whined at than withstood'. I regard it as largely peripheral. St Helens was a large Christian Broth-ers Novitiate at the end of our road. The young boys took their Sun-day constitutional in groups of three. I heard later, this was to prevent inappropriate relationships. It closed in the 70s and is now a luxury hotel. 'Quinsy' is more of a chancy thing, one thought borrowing an-other, ending with three 'X's'—kiss, illiterate signature, error.

'Working for the Government', the title poem of the second book, has something again of that faceless, nameless agent. But here the setting seems to be the West of Ireland, like so many of your poems. What's the gravitational pull there, both actually and in the poems? Also, money is invoked. I'm probably wrong, but much of the imagery at the heart of the poem seems to derive obliquely from the Sean Lemass soundbite about the rising tide that lifts all boats in relation to economics. I suppose, as with the other poets in the anthology, I am interested in those moments where the so-called Celtic Tiger is visible in the poem.

However naively, I thought Sean Lemass was modern and good for the country, though I know some people now take the view that the opening up in the 60s would have happened anyway. I started working in the 70s, a pre-computer age where all enquiries were sent by post, work entered in ledgers, carbon copies filed etc. etc. In my first year in the job I was transferred round the country at a day's notice and for a suburban boy this orientation (disorientation?) was initially great fun, but ultimately became banal and tedious.

One of my first stints was to Clifden in Co. Galway. I was required to find and visit isolated farmers for various government schemes. The landscape just seemed to make sense, extraordinary light and color with no shouting for attention. Tim Robinson, the author and cartographer based in Roundstone, captures it brilliantly. Also Eamon Grennan in his poetry. The more you visit, of course, the more contacts and specific places resonate.

'Offering the Light', the first in Water & Power, is a really beautiful little nugget. But, like many of your poems, it does need some unraveling. On the most basic level, can you explain the cricket terminology to a US audience and your attraction to it? It reminds me greatly of the gorgeous Douglas Dunn poem 'Close of Play', where cricketers leaving the field are likened to ghosts. Was this image evocative of a vanishing

world for you as well? More specifically, what's the allure of dusk as a metaphor? Also, this wonderful idea at the end that the truest map of a place is the place itself; that a thing is its own best metaphor. Your rhyme 'Dublin' with 'Dublin'!

I liked Roy Harper's early 70s hit, 'When an old Cricketer Leaves the Crease'—close of play, dusk gathering and a fleeting glimpse of a twelfth man at silly mid-on. The poem uses a few cricketing terms. It's about a five-day test match and play can be halted for a number of reasons. Rain, failing light, etc. Batsmen under pressure like the idea of abandoning play for the day. The quality of light can trigger the five lights on the pavilion wall to come on in sequence and when three are lit the umpires will 'offer the light to the batsmen'. The 'nightwatchman' is a safe pair of hands, put in to bat, near dusk, to guide the team safely through until the next day. Silly point is a field position close to the batsman and so, considered somewhat dangerous. There are, of course, some parallels with baseball. The final map image recalls a Borges short story. I liked the image of the dutiful/obsessive servant told to draw up a map of the city and as more and more details accumulate, the scale rises inexorably.

Can I ask you to explain the narrative of 'The Railway Guard'? What's happening in the poem? Can I ask you to say something, again, about the structure of the poem, how that impressionism of the passing landscape that the poem is flitting through is created by image running into image, stanza into stanza? I think there are only five sentences in a poem that's thirty-six lines long. This and 'Stoney Road' feel close too in their attention to inherited landscapes.

It's one of those returning poems, years on and out of season. Our transience, fleeting traces left in soil deposits and grasses. In 1957 there was an explosion at the British nuclear power plant in Windscale (renamed Sellafield) so there is a reference to Geiger boys. News was more controlled then and we heard nothing of any threat to milk supplies, food, swimming, etc. There are the printed images of those summers fading to white and a memory of a beloved, smiling, silent niece joining my grandfather—who was the Station Master/Railway Guard in Drogheda—and who I remember visiting when I was four or five. He rose to greet me from his fireside chair, white hair, white whiskers, surrounded by a plume of white pipe smoke. It's the only image I have of him. 'Stoney Road' is a last image of my mother in old age praying for release. She had had enough.

'From Portstewart to Portrush' is real Derek Mahon territory, not just geographically, but also in how it celebrates the 'debt to pleasure in the mundane'. Our generation owes so much to Mahon, doesn't it? In a way that might not be immediately obvious to those outside of Ireland. Can I ask you to say something about him, his work, its impact on yours, and what you think he has added uniquely to Irish poetry?

In 1998 there was a three-day conference on Derek Mahon at the University of Ulster in Coleraine. My brother was going up and I joined him on a whim. It was a small gathering, young academics on the make, like one of Mahon's own strange sects in 'Nostalgias'—'In a tiny stone church / On a desolate headland / a lost tribe is singing "Abide with me".' Actually it was fun—though I found myself (like at school) staring out the window at the routine rural doings and a commuter train plying its trade, back and forth between neighboring towns.

Mahon is now over 70 and yet there is remarkably little written about him. Like Thomas Kinsella, he is *sui generis*, the real thing. His tone is immaculate; he has a wickedly sly sense of humor and is a wonderful reader of his own work. He has led an admirable maverick existence outside the comforts of the paycheck and pension, and if you stick rigorously to the poems, he is an example to us all.

Cinema is very important to you, isn't it? One poem references Michael Cimino's ill-fated Heaven's Gate. The title poem of your third book, though about your father's watch and its demise while swimming, does also seem to draw on Roman Polanski's Chinatown! Is this way wide of the mark? Isn't Water & Power the LA civic authority that Jack Nicholson is investigating? More generally, where do these references fit?

Suburban cinemas were the norm in the 50s and 60s and my father used to bring me and my younger brother every week to the local Stella until we could go on our own. In 1969 I went to University College Dublin in Earlsfort Terrace, and joined the film society. This was a crash course in recent and classic European/World cinema— Truffaut, Godard, Antonioni, Jancso, Forman, Malle, Bergman, Kurosawa etc. It was a perfect grounding for the marvelous new wave American films of the 70s and 80s. I liked *Heaven's Gate* even if it was a little overwrought. Its intended six-hour length might have done it justice. Like Welles' *The Magnificent Ambersons*, the studio butchered it in a vain attempt to recoup costs. And *Chinatown* is a marvelous film, everyone on top of their game and a wonderful script. And you're right: the doomed Hollis Mulwray is the chief of the Water & Power Department. Corruption is a constant, but self deception is somehow more interesting.

Can I ask you to say something about the form of 'Everything In Its Place', which seems to hover loosely between terza rima and villanelle? How does that connect, also, with what this poem (or any poem) is about? Those flush central rhymes kind of enact the rod mining for samples. More generally, what's your thinking of rhymes and stanzas? Do you decide before the poem begins, or does it happen naturally during composition?

For me, form nearly always asserts itself. There was a vogue a while ago for sestinas and villanelles. They all seemed very pleased with themselves in magazines etc., though somehow, the end result appeared worthy rather than the real thing. Mahon published an early villanelle, 'Antarctica', which is sensational. If you can't get that formal elegance and lightness of touch, it seems pointless. Sometimes in the attempt to complete a poem, rhymes and stanzas become insistent (or don't as the case may be). You can keep rewriting to avoid what might be a straightjacket, but form often persists and finally becomes a release. So 'Everything in Its Place' attempts a loose musical rhythm. A guy in a skyscraper looks out at a building next door under construction, with a kind of inverted mining imagery. The rhyme simply fell into place.

Both 'The Cancer Bureau' and 'Quince', though the latter insists on non-belief, read as being as much about faith as anything more literal. Are poems acts, or paradigms, of faith for you?

Paradigms of faith may be a bit lofty for me, but perhaps if one eschews 'that vast, moth-eaten musical brocade' of faith religion, you end up clinging to the wreckage of something else, then something else again. In 'The Cancer Bureau' I loved the idea of the Load line and the Plimsol mark, simple visual aids indicating cargo load. And the hospital nurse, casually drawing lines and tattoos on the body, diagnoses and balance. The poem ends with a faith in the world, as is. 'Quince' makes fun of the New Year resolution to get out more, plant more exotically and live off the consequences. If there is a sense of faith here, it's in weather and seasons.

Of the new poems included, both 'An Old Boyne Fish Barn' and 'Tate Water' seem to be about water and seeing. They dwell on the weight of things, whether it is 'the weight of water' or 'the weight of . . . vision'. I have asked the other poets this, so perhaps should ask you as well: what is the draw to light and water in your work?

I think we are a wee bit obsessed with both in these parts. The Boyne is a famous salmon run. What returns with each tide however is complicated by some 60-year-old leakage from Second World War munitions dumps in the Irish Sea. In 'Tate Water' the focus is more that water has no color in itself, but depends on various forms of light, though the putative narrator ties himself up in his own hubris and leaves the conclusion hanging. It could be more for a painter's eye, but that doesn't stop you trying to catch some of that rich transience. And it's where I live, the sea nearly always in view, the memory of foghorns, a cruel history of ship wreck and drowning and the harbor at Dun Laoghaire with its relics of empire and emigration. The changing light now seems less a feature of what we live in and more of a miracle, to be celebrated out of the everyday.

There are also two beautiful love poems: 'A Love Poem' and 'In My Reading'. Both, though very different, seem to celebrate a wide-eyed innocence of seeing things as if for the first time. They also attempt to reconcile the world we do see and that glimpsed through borrowed sight, whether it be 'Mir's captain' or in books. Is there, do you think, a clearer celebratory note in your newer work? And can you say something about the difficulty of writing love poems?

Innocence seems correct, rather than a world weary stale view. It's a tricky business though, and if it emerges as such, it seems more comfortable if it can exist of its own accord rather than carrying too much freight. Both these poems are simple enough, leaning a bit on whatever was to hand. If some poems take a few years to come into an acceptable focus and form, so be it. And if I'm celebrating anything, it's the joy of persistence.

Finally, can you say something about how you write a poem? Has it changed much over the years? Or is this something you prefer not to think about?

I do admire those who can plan the piece beforehand, set the parameters and style and with talent and discipline come up with the goods. My efforts are more like the child past bedtime, insisting on yet another glass of water. (We are back to 'water' again!) I think you once told me you like to get the correct last line. Maybe a bit too high-wire for me. But I think it's still true; you can get a line on a bus, a line staring out a window, a line of speech—something to get you going, and that could be some peace or a clattery café, and then there's music or rereading some poet who never disappoints. If I usually start with quite a long first draft I will often have to go back months later to find the original spark. So I still write in longhand. The pattern hasn't changed much and I wouldn't want to analyze it much either.

WAITING ON LEMASS

It is nineteen sixty two
Or three, and we are playing soccer
In fields laced with the sheen of bamboo.

In the air that turns
Amber like sally rods,
Somewhere out of picture,

A man is hitting golf balls
As if there were no tomorrow.
He slouches towards the sycamore shade

Searching for what couples
Might be lying in the seed beds
Or that tall grass

Loosely flecked with rye.
None the wiser, we walk home
Under the beige satellites

That roll in the ether of themselves,
While all about,
A blaze of radio perfume

Speaks of a man
Moving his ships on soup-like waters,
Or a president slumped

On his girlfriend's knee,
As here our long druid leaders
Wander through the closing zones,

Their autistic god
Commanding options in the street,
The curfew till the white hour.

MAKING DEALS

Landscape painters, photographers,
have us standing awkwardly
ignoring the image maker—
it's only half a lie,

for we are the ciphers
that give you what you see.

All round the growing cold streets
men are making deals.
They meet in bars, hush,
bend heads and gesture

in the underhand.
Within their splayed fingers
the cluttered microfilm exchange
of blueprints passed

all in the ease
of casual conversation.

Where we made the streets
gaps became alleyways
and men rode out in cars
to marshal the intelligence

of addresses. Now as money
abandons the derelict sites
they circle on stilts
attempting to cohere the subterfuge.

Watch as the centre slowly hollows
and cables map the countryside.

PHILBY IN IRELAND

Nightfall, and we have driven out
From the warm lights. The thick fog
Circling the hill's base, corrodes
Our white car as it stalks the incline.

From this high air we can see
The crawling streets, trucks and buses
Wheeling in their correct motions—
Trails leaving a decipher of rests.

Somewhere in this parallel of workings
Men catalogue the labyrinth of the city
And deep in its crushed underbelly
We meet and copy the blueprints

Of a world drawn out on long papers,
Lives collapse if we fail, for our work
Though underhand, is significant,
Like priests we are diligent or we do not

Believe. Abandoning cars, we move down
To the murmuring inlets, wide lagoons
Cheeping at the breaker wall. We sail out
Adrift in the wider perspective.

THE FINAL MANOEUVRE

Living the middle life
Caught between lovers
I was prepared for the holocaust

That never came.
Crossing years like days
On a schoolboy's calendar

Tracking without retreat
I was the inexorable traveller
Pursuing my wounded grail.

On that chill November evening
In Glenmalure, I could have owned
The whole of Wicklow

But fences would have encouraged thieves.
So, turning now in this cocoon
of soft noises

I stare smiling
Toward the spark of the living,
Their coloured flags weaving

A cosy fever, their loves
Chased by clock-hands
And a life's debris.

Lying in this damp chair
A festering in the moor-swamp's side
I draw a pulled curtain of hair

To keep the seasons in ebb-tide;
While this axle of earth
Conceals me, composes my relief.

CHEMOTHERAPY

Tensing on the trip-switch of mustard gas
A pillow smell can now set off distress.
The nurse rounding my corridor of glass
Holds her neat tray, her lipped capsule's largesse.

MATT KIERNAN

He tries to explain
How a gift emerges
Singing from the shadows,

How holding the reamer like a baton
Conducts receding melodies,

And how rhythm runs
Like a finger through a stencil in his brain.

The radio light trembles,
And the battery bleeds in its cage,
So when at last he plays

The air is as true
As the quiet inflection of easter snow
Settling in its drifts of blue.

TRAVELLING LIGHT

Before Christmas, the small gatherings
In banks and corporate offices, afterhours,
Mime the end-of-year parties.

I watch a brave middle-income troupe
In St Martin-in-the-Fields
Rehearse the *St Matthew Passion,*

Unseasonal scores, a birth not a death,
And momentarily forgotten,
Their cars, their frail insignia,

Speed underground back
To the flotilla of wharfs and gardens,
Where threadbare estate lines

Haphazardly define that otherness
From me, and these drowsy London Irish tramps,
Who stretch and snore in the heated pews.

When, head in hand, your face emerges,
A young woman invoking the Messiah—
Blond neck bare, strings of beads

Rolled between the lynx light hairs—
I relax to imbibe that phrasing,
Performed time and time over

Like instinct or a commandment,
And know these sometimes lines are the ties
That will reluctantly, if eventually, define.

JULY IN BETTYSTOWN

When the linen flaps open
With its east coast view of the Mournes,
And Ian Fleming novelettes
Hide in a pile of fragrant clothes,

There is always the sea—
That reeling silence on a line,
And the clay like ground tarragon,
With its stench of burnished brine.

And always the hint of fire,
The thatch in its myriad parts,
And the air full of black-tailed grass
That some times has red hearts.

THE FIFTIES PARENT

When he smiled, Khrushchev hovered towards me,
Airbrushing days with bliss,

And his bald baby's wrinkled face
Was almost touching, almost miming a kiss.

MURPHY'S HEXAGON REVISITED

i.m. Patrick King

Ten years after our March race across Ireland to Omey,
Volkswagen replaced by a Renault, I visit the hexagon alone.
Through a stumbling graveyard, past a couple saving hay
In this wet summer's one God-given-day.

Fifteen hands high it appears to stand,
Like an old English thruppence weeping bronze into sand.

And though beguiled in its space—a dovetail net of mercy—
The sloped bed, stove and desk, covet the margins of sea.

But who owns this washing line, these lazy beds that curl,
The zigzag of hedging as the light bars unfurl?
And is this a right-of-way, did I walk across or drive,
Is this the latitude, the one day the sea does not arrive?

LEAVING ST HELENS

The swarm of black-clad novices
Walking past our door
In groups of three

Vanished overnight.
Now as fields
Fill with rape

And the perfumed garden
Reverts to pasture,
The great house resembles

An impromptu barracks.
A world is being
Mobilised or demobbed,

Doors flung open,
Moon-dazed clocks
Running fast—

And like sappers
Lost in the North Wood
We lean to the right

Listening for our balance
While the earth drags
Beneath our feet.

Time is moving away.
It happens like that.
People lose interest.

QUINSY

Imagining I had quinsy
I gave the grass a quiff
where it was turning to meadow.

But just as a fever
curls in its own smoke
I found it hard to swallow,

that a guillemot
blown off course
could succumb to rumor,

or eyeing sweet william
in my thatch of garden,
come down on the side of caution.

And I could be his nemesis,
his thorn, his briar,
though I could as well

resemble the red kite
ghosting a saraband
through the Coto Doñana,

as I know my nurse
who tethers the spatula
will tease the cipherings

of bile and sand,
while we search for the kiss,
the signature, the error.

SHE SCRATCHES HIS WRIST

She scratches his wrist once or twice
They tell in signals of their private vice.

I am a witness, not some eye from above
Some things we do not know, or only tell in love.

WORKING FOR THE GOVERNMENT

Walking these cut-throat fields
Far from the latest outrage,
My thin-lipped parchments

Show the short, sharp inlets
Where the Atlantic blares.
In the drone and swathe of meetings
We tell how money allocates,
How long corridors
Stretch into the lime of mid-evening
And how chimes rise and bathe
Like a submerged village of commerce
Hanging onto the edge of the world.
Now we have only distance—
Documents on deal tables,
A feathery importance mumbling
Incoherences, as here in Easter Week
I rewrite the cloven, haphazard
Labyrinth of the order of my life.
Hardly the stuff of obituaries!

OFFERING THE LIGHT

If three white on the score board
should lead to an offer
to abandon the day's endeavour,
I'll play the night watchman

who heads for the pavilion
taking with me
a last glance round silly point,
a brief sweep of boundary and bye

and one more entry
for that loose archive,
where the real map of Dublin
is about the same size as Dublin.

THE RAILWAY GUARD

Past the church, a brambled lane,
the remains of dairy farms,
legal notes hammered onto fence posts
and fields of assorted grasses

burning clear to the iron track.
Out of this dry clay near Gormanston,
in the needle white of November,
men still bring their horses down

to hug the foreshore
as if what they fear in the encroaching tide
is not the tide alone.
Moon worshippers used to winter here,

and their bitumen chalets,
in vapours of creosote,
now lie chalk-pegged for the Geiger boys
so all our bruised affection

bristles in cardoons and docks.
From such marine enamel,

sandy scores of the black and the white
might tell how we recede

in the scant world
of the bled photogravure,
but Clare smiles and whispers
that here is as good as anywhere

to mimic the salmon shoals
who never betray
what gossip might thrive
in the olive orchards and seaweed barrios.

I know that fifteen summers
spent on my knees, combing through
eel grass, sea holly, sea lavender,
could never hope to appease,

but when she walks to greet
my grandfather—the railway guard—
on his Marsh Road settee,
she is whiter than all of these.

STONEY ROAD

Tell me once more what she said as she lay
On the polished bed of anthracite, cool to the touch—
You'll pray that I am taken from this house, one day—
As if words alone could ask for so much.

THE CANCER BUREAU

The nurse paints on my puffed belly
The Load line or the Plimsol mark.
She says it will rise and fall through salt water
And where tidal streams
Connive to build their rudimentary dreams,
She says my weight will be greater.
So much for the spindles, pulleys and shafts
Who conspire to show
My maximum permitted loading
For Winter North Atlantic, Indian Summer
And Tropical Fresh Water,
For as I tell her over and over,
I never plan to leave this world again.

QUINCE

For my new year resolution
I'll plant quince

in the boggy warren of the garden,
or in pots, trailing somewhat

but giving up their fat, like pears.
I'll spend autumn sniffing

the peachy down, on their soft baby heads,
place them in a bowl for pomander,

then scrape what fragrance comes
from the puckered leaves

to rub on my nonexistent spleen.
I may need a cure for dropsy,

a balm for the asthmatic lung,
something to place on the red

that inflames my eyes,
but, as forbidden fruit takes on

the fulsome curve of a dwarf cello,
I'll remain in the suit

of the man who flits
from roulade to madeleine,

conversant with all faiths
and believing in none.

WATER AND POWER

My father's watch
was the only thing I wore
when I dived into the Merrimack
in the summer of 1974.

An engagement present—
it seized with rust
faster than I could grapple
with the ties of trust.

I had let slip the role
that love plays
in a sketch or a rectangle,
and though it had some way

to tease the future,
I was unaware
of such swift currents
nor could I dare

to travel too far out
towards the wooden pins
following their line
in the racing mill.

Even if I could jump
into the same river twice,
so the watch could regain
what it was once,

how can I mourn a proof
for shock and dust
when water and power
are what needs must.

A LOVE STORY

Last night we camped
on Boss Croker's acres,
tonight we cross
a river in spate,

in the miles between
a white-haired man
carries his gospel of brake-
pads and corrugated iron

like the sheets of asbestos
which we found to our cost
when we tramped
through Kippure and Ticknock.

We cough in unison,
we argue over direction
and though we had come
in search of rue des Favorites,

to take on the low down
of its honky-tonk bars,
we bear witness to unnamed
toxins, the *domestique*

who gestures like a friend,
as the halting ambition
that dithers and skews
and is brought to its knees

lets us gaze again
on brownfield and edgeland,
with all the aplomb
of Mir's captain.

IN MY READING

If there is such a thing anymore
as a humble servant in the vineyard

this is he, a man from the coast
home on his lunch break

working the stooped enclosure
below me as I read and revel

in the feral words of murder
on what passes for a roof garden

with a view of Pompeii
and further below

through French doors,
you sleeping, an afternoon to dream

or pray after the heat of love making,
just as his turning broken clay

with a method learned as a boy
becomes a kind of recreation

to justify and while away
olive baskets filled with autumn

as his mother, who once
combed her hair like Myrna Loy,

watches with approval
this noise of renewal

or so it appears
in my reading.

TATE WATER

If you ask how a colour might come about
consider the enigma of water determined by sky,
and by water I don't mean pool or rain barrel
but the wide expanse of sea or lake.
As with all things, this will depend
on where and when you look
because water absorbs light, and sea water
absorbs the larger truths of late evening
greater than the timid blue of morning.
So if sunlight entering the sea is filtered
until mainly blue and then washed back
to the observer above, who could be you
dawdling on cliff or private promontory,
then like you, a stain of light depends on impurity
just as your purplish skin for cold or bruise

like a Doppler note, brightens and passes and fades.
And if pine lakes deliver a bluish tinge,
remember in that water, increasing salts or acids
can make of the scattered light a trawl from pale
yellow to darkish brown and when peat is washed
down, sunlight may lose itself, cannot scatter
and the lake becomes black. I can tell you,
impasto giving weight, how to make a profession
of mute things, but remain at a loss to figure
how the weight of water can be so sinister.

AN OLD BOYNE FISH BARN

You should have seen the sea in those days,
wind smoke and weeping flares washing

ashore from the barrios, all those
hesitant evacuees, as tarpaulin stretched

along Beaufort's Dyke and our drift nets
sailed through the Hebrides. Shuffling in pipe

smoke, scribbling a plume of grave longing
on the bones of a wax-bright dusk,

I stood to see the ranks at the fish barn—
open mouthed, open boxed, iced on shelf

after shelf—and stayed to inhabit
what remains for the solipsistic raconteur

who believes the weight of his vision
will dissolve with his last sigh. When I drag

a heavy catch out of the evening,
old weather, braced for meteorites,

groans like a dehumidifier and burbles
the gospel of faith and love and water.

PERMISSIONS

The editors gratefully acknowledge the permission of these writers and publishers to reprint the material in this book:

COLETTE BRYCE Poems from *The Heel of the Bernadette*, *The Full Indian Rope Trick*, and *Self-Portrait in the Dark* reprinted with the permission of Macmillan. "Boredoom" and "Jean" are reprinted with the permission of the Author.

JUSTIN QUINN Poems from *The 'O'o'a'a' Bird* and *Privacy* are reprinted with the permission of Carcanet Press. Poems from *Fuselage*, *Waves and Trees*, and *Close Quarters* are reprinted with the permission of The Gallery Press. "Nostalgia" is reprinted with the permission of the Author.

JOHN MCAULIFFE Poems from *A Better Life*, *Next Door*, and *Of All Places* are reprinted with the permission of The Gallery Press.

MAURICE RIORDAN Poems from *A Word from the Loki*, *Floods*, and *The Holy Land* are reprinted with the permission of Faber and Faber. "The Dun Cow," "Stars and Jasmine," and "The Nests" are reprinted with the permission of the Author.

GERARD FANNING Poems from *Easter Snow*, *Working for the Government*, and *Water & Power* are reprinted with the permission of Dedalus Press. "A Love Story," "In My Reading," "Tate Water," and "An Old Boyne Fishing Barn" are reprinted with the permission of the Author.